STILL LIFE

frontispiece photograph by Nem Elliott

STILL LIFE

The Story of a Struggle with Disablement

by

ELIZABETH TWISTINGTON HIGGINS

LONDON
A. R. MOWBRAY & CO LTD

© *Elizabeth Twistington Higgins, 1969*
*Printed in Great Britain by
Alden & Mowbray Ltd
at the Alden Press, Oxford*
SBN 264 64504 9
First published in 1969

CONTENTS

	Preface	*page* xi
	Foreword by Dame Ninette de Valois	xiii
1	CHILDHOOD AND SCHOOLDAYS	1
2	FIRST CAREER: THE BALLET	10
3	THE THEATRE	18
4	POLIO STRIKES	26
5	IN THE IRON LUNG	33
6	SECOND CAREER: MOUTH PAINTING	51
7	THE WAY OUT	58
8	TELEVISION	64
9	I GO TO SEA	73
10	A PLACE OF MY OWN	108
11	FULL CIRCLE	115
12	EPILOGUE	120

ACKNOWLEDGEMENTS

To my father who wrote the Preface in 1964, hoping that I would eventually write this book.

I am greatly indebted also to Dr. N. E. Cameron for hours of help and advice; and to Mrs. Alan Bailey for invaluable assistance.

My very grateful thanks to Dame Ninette de Valois who has contributed the Foreword; to Canon William Purcell, literary advisor to A. R. Mowbray & Co. Ltd., for his guidance and encouragement; and to Jaqueline Basford, my secretary, who has worked devotedly and with great patience.

Also to Miss Merlyn Severn, Mrs. Nem Elliott and Mr. Peter Russell for their generous help with the photographs.

I have received valuable assistance from many people, especially my helpers who set me up to work each day. Without their aid I could achieve nothing.

To all those who have
helped me to live again

Oft he seems to hide his face,
But unexpectedly returns...
Milton

PREFACE

POLIOMYELITIS, variously styled in virtue of its technical characteristics Anterior Poliomyelitis, Polio-encephalitis, Infantile Paralysis, for generations one of the gravest scourges of mankind, has now been conquered. The long-cherished dream has come true. The causal virus has been discovered and by a simple process of immunisation, the disease can be prevented. If the facilities for prevention be rigorously utilized, there need be no more 'Polio'.

But this crowning achievement is recent history and, unfortunately for many, it came too late. Thus former victims of Polio are left with us to cope, as best they can, with their varying degrees of disability. For the majority this may not be too difficult. For the few who have been less lucky, the problems can be well-nigh overwhelming. To solve them to the utmost possible demands supreme skill and dauntless courage. The triumphs have an epic quality.

This autobiographical sketch of the struggles of a ballet dancer and teacher to become a mouth painter, must surely interest all who can appreciate and salute high spiritual fortitude and accomplishment in the face of dire physical calamity.

Thomas Twistington Higgins F.R.C.S.

FOREWORD

'THE discipline has been good for me . . .'

In this sentence in her Epilogue Elizabeth sums up the dedicated simplicity that dancers all share. Our profession is known in the theatre to be the most highly disciplined, and here we have an artist's cry from the heart, after years of physical pain and mental suffering that removed her from her chosen career.

It is a statement that might well, because of its very lack of bravura, self-pity and arrogance, act as shock treatment to those who would abandon all 'discipline' for a no-man's land of their own making. Elizabeth's no-man's land was thrust upon her and she accepted it, was prepared to weigh it up, and with the aid of self-control was not in the end to find it wanting.

Because of its lack of self-pity, sentimentality and false values, this book is deeply moving; there are shafts of pure wisdom in some of her reflections and I quote the following as an example: 'Accepting a disability is an *act* of faith—not a loss of faith.'

She never descends to sketching herself as a plaster saint; her temperament, with its ups and downs, is dealt with in an astonishingly frank way; she fought for her creative urge to be satisfied; she fought openly, aggressively if necessary, but always within the limits of behaviour that one would only expect to find in someone with no physical handicaps.

Sitting with her in her room in Walmer one afternoon, I was suddenly made acutely aware of a great force in her life—her father. It was a chance remark on Elizabeth's part, but for me a curtain parted, letting in a flood of light.

'You know,' she said, 'my father made it clear to me one day. He said, "Never forget you are exactly the same as everyone else, except for the fact that you cannot move." '

She went through with a busy, fruitful life just accepting this one single fact—she could not move. There it ended, everything else was intact; a 'Still Life' to be lived to the full, within and without.

She has done it, and so is the pride of every dancer and dance student in the world.

> 'Henceforth I ask not good fortune—I myself am good fortune;
> Henceforth I whimper no more, postpone no more, need nothing,
> Strong and content, I travel the open road . . .'

Elizabeth's life is a 'Song of the Open Road' as was Walt Whitman's poem.

Ninette de Valois, D.B.E.

I

CHILDHOOD AND SCHOOLDAYS

My appearance in the world coincided with the midnight chimes of 5 November, the night when we commemorate the discovery of the plot to blow up the Houses of Parliament and the arrest of the traitor Guy Fawkes. My birthday, therefore, is always heralded by conflagrations and fireworks.

When I was born, in 1923, my parents were living in a terraced house overlooking London's Primrose Hill. They already had two children—Ian, four years old, and Janet a year younger.

My mother, Jessie Ingram, was of Scottish descent. Her parents and grandparents were schoolteachers and her sister followed in their footsteps. Both her brothers became doctors, and she herself became a nurse.

My paternal grandparents were Irish, settling down in this country at the beginning of the century. Grandfather was a Protestant Vicar in Cheshire, and it was from here that my father won a scholarship to the Manchester Grammar School. He went on to do his medical training at the Infirmary and became a Fellow of the Royal College of Surgeons at an incredibly early age. During the first world war, he and my mother met whilst serving in the Army in France.

At the time of my birth, my father was gradually establishing a practice in London and was to make a name for himself as a pioneer of children's surgery. Although he was working at various London hospitals, most of his time was devoted to the Hospital for Sick Children, Great Ormond Street.

When I was two, we moved to Well Walk near Hampstead Heath. The house was ugly but the large, walled-in garden behind it made a perfect playground for us children. The garage at the end of this had a playroom-cum-garden-shed attached where we played happily and fairly safely.

My earliest recollection concerns this room. I was a plump, rosy-faced child with long golden ringlets and was always bursting into tears at the slightest provocation. I remember toddling through the conservatory from the garden into the drawing-room. To my small stature the room seemed enormous. My mother was sitting at the far end by the fire, and as I approached, her face took on a look of horror.

'Betty!' she exclaimed. 'What has happened to your nice curls?'

Immediately, I started to howl. I had no idea when I had been playing 'hairdressers' in the garden shed that Ian had lopped them off with the hedge clippers! My hair has been completely straight ever since.

I do not remember the arrival of my brother Robin. He and Nanny joined the family when I was about fourteen months old. Nanny was rather prim and very English. She was small, with round red cheeks and straight dark hair closely plaited round her ears in the 'ear-phone' style. When this style went out of fashion, I used to watch fascinated as her hairdresser marcel-waved her hair, heating the tongs over the gas ring in the night nursery. Occasionally, there was the added horror of the singeing treatment, when I thought her hair was going to disappear in a burst of flames. Nanny always said that she preferred little boys and Robin was obviously a favourite. She told me later that I was very jealous of the new baby and once tried to bite off his little toe!

I retain only snapshot memories of the time we spent in Hampstead; Ian with both hands covered in big brown furry caterpillars; my mother, pushing the pram through a thunderstorm on the Heath and in her hurry spraining her ankle; our neighbours throwing us sweets over the garden wall; and

Robin, only three years old, pretending to drive me in the car, twisting the wheel, honking the horn, fidgeting with the gears and crashing us straight into the garage wall!

My sister Brighid was born in July 1928, and later that year we moved to a large block of flats in Harley Street. It seemed cramped after the freedom of Hampstead, but it was only a temporary home. I celebrated my sixth birthday here and this was definitely a highlight in my life, possibly because I was allowed to choose my own present—a lovely dark red dolls' pram. I was also allowed to choose my birthday lunch —turkey and sausages, peaches and cream—in fact, this was my birthday menu for several years to come.

Janet and I went to Francis Holland School. I dreaded it because I was frightened of being left there; I was sure Nanny would forget to fetch me. When I could be persuaded to forget this fear, I quite enjoyed myself, especially the handwork classes. I think I inherited my great love of this from my grandmothers and great-grandmothers who made colourful patchwork quilts, Irish crochet, hand-made lace, fine white embroidery, and old-fashioned baby clothes tucked and frilled and embroidered. Much of their exquisite creations are still used today, heirlooms that remind us of a more leisurely age.

The worst afternoon of my week was Friday when I had to go to a dancing class. This was given by a rather fierce lady, all legs and gym slip, who taught remedial exercises and gymnastics as well. I remember little else about these classes, except that I was always freezing cold in my blue silk dress. I must have shown some aptitude, however, as the teacher thought I should be trained to be a dancer. My parents strongly disapproved and, I am told, *I* met the suggestion with tearful protests. The matter was dropped.

Soon we moved to the other end of Harley Street. This house was typical of this part of London—five stories and a basement. The rooms were large and beautifully proportioned, with huge windows, high ceilings and Adam mantelpieces. Janet and I shared a bedroom at the top. It was a terrifying journey from the nursery up to bed, past the gurgling water tank at the end of our landing. I used to do it at top speed lest a demon should pounce out on me.

The family was completed in November 1930 with the arrival of Alison. The morning after she was born, I was eating my elevenses at school when the teacher said, 'The Headmistress would like to see you.'

She led me without more ado to her room at the end of the corridor. After knocking on the door, she pushed me in and left.

I found myself in a small, book-lined room which seemed to be filled by the rotund figure of the Headmistress.

'What have you got to tell me dear?' she asked, patting my head.

My mouth was still full of biscuit which I was too nervous to chew, and I, remembering that it was rude to speak with my mouth full, just nodded.

'Did you get a new baby sister last night?' she said.

Again I nodded, and that was the sum total of our conversation. She must have thought me a very dumb pupil.

When I was eight I went to the new Junior St. Paul's Girls' school. It was beautifully equipped and the newness of it all appealed to me.

One lesson in particular made a deep impression. Gustav Holst, the Musical Director of the Senior school, came to teach us singing. He was a slender, shy man with tremendous vivacity, peering out at the world short-sightedly through small, steel-rimmed spectacles with pebble lenses. Although there were only about twelve of us in the class, he got tremendously excited conducting us, willing us to come in on time and insisting on very clear enunciation. He must have

CHILDHOOD AND SCHOOLDAYS

been a marvellous teacher to have made such an impression on one so young. Unfortunately, he had died by the time I graduated to the Senior school, so this was the only time I sang under his baton. It was a great privilege and joy and a very precious memory.

Occasionally, I read the lesson at prayers and once made an appeal on behalf of Great Ormond Street hospital. In this, I told my fellow pupils how much these poor children needed the money 'as the walls of the hospital were falling down!' I was a bit disconcerted at the laughter that followed this remark, but the financial results were good. I learnt Greek dancing and found I was one of the best in the class. I enjoyed the games and the gymnastics, the sewing and handwork, but showed little distinction in the academic subjects.

However, I was bright enough to pass the entrance examination into the Senior School, which was richly endowed with extensive and beautiful buildings; a new science wing, an indoor heated swimming pool, and a magnificent music wing where teachers worked in sound-proofed rooms. There I had piano lessons from a ferocious, fat Polish lady. My lessons came immediately after lunch and I always found her drinking hot water as, she said, coffee was fattening. She was an excellent pianist however, and I became adept at persuading her to play to me on the days when I had done little or no practice and was thus spared her well-deserved reprimands, if I was lucky.

I was allowed to sew in the art classes as I enjoyed this more than painting and drawing, and the only prize I ever won was for needlework. Here too, I was good at games and gym but otherwise an unspectacular pupil.

. . . . .

My mother must have had a very difficult household to organise, but to us everything seemed to run smoothly in spite of frequent changes of domestic staff. Nanny presided over the nursery for nearly eighteen years and we had a secure and very orderly life. We were taken to school by car, often leaving Father en route at one of the hospitals or nursing homes. He started operating very early in the morning and worked exceedingly long hours. Often, the waiting room was full of patients when we got home at about five o'clock and we would creep past the consulting room and up to the nursery.

Perhaps we had less freedom and independence than children living in the country, but we had many other advantages. In spite of their busy lives, our parents found time to take us to the Museums and Art Galleries where we absorbed much useful knowledge which, nowadays, is brought into the home by means of television. Nanny walked us for miles through the parks and streets and we came to know our London intimately.

We made our own entertainment. From an early age we each learnt a musical instrument, and together formed a small family orchestra. The boys played the piano, Janet the flute, Brighid the cello; I played the violin and Alison, who was only three, the drum. The resulting din often brought telephone calls from the neighbours requesting us to close the windows! The boys were really gifted, especially Robin. (He later became a choral scholar at King's College, Cambridge, and took Part I of his Bachelor of Music degree whilst studying Medicine.) He sight-read with great facility. When he and I sang together, he helped me with my part, sang his own and played the piano accompaniment all at sight. He was only ten!

We also had a lot of fun with our theatrical performances, charades and our Christmas pantomime. Every year, Father wrote this himself and rehearsed us and we performed to Mother, Nanny and anybody else willing to be an audience.

I don't know how he found time to write these pantomimes but he did, and, I think, probably enjoyed acting in them as much as we did. We kept a dressing-up trunk which, through the years, had acquired all types of costumes; ribbons, flowers, old hats and other oddments. Burnt cork featured much in these performances and each year, Ian, invariably the villain of the piece, found an excuse to black out some of his teeth. I don't think we were very good actors, but our performances caused much hilarity.

Once a week now, a dancing class was held in our drawing-room when six other children joined us to learn ballet. We were taught by a surgeon's wife—a tall, jolly, vivacious person, though a very good disciplinarian. She brought her own pianist and I think we all enjoyed the lessons. For myself, I derived great pleasure from moving to music but found the preliminary barre exercises very irksome. There were so many things to remember simultaneously that I used to get rather exasperated with myself. It seemed almost impossible for me to keep my head up, shoulders down, tummy in, legs turned out, knees straight and toes pointed, all at the same time. I was too young to appreciate the importance of good teaching and the acquisition of a sound technique.

My father felt the need of a country house for us and bought a large, rambling one in Kent. It was full of character; oak panelling and beams, and open fireplaces where we had roaring log fires. A previous owner had added an extra wing—the ground floor consisting of one enormous room like a ball-room, with a beautiful parquet floor and windows on two sides overlooking the garden. We used this as a play-room and had plenty of space to let off steam.

There were several acres of garden, with orchards and greenhouses filled with vines, and for two glorious months every summer we had a taste of real freedom. We played tennis, croquet and endless imaginative games. There was a

Wendy house in the garden and, in no time at all, I was running a Wendy house school. I must have been the bane of my young sisters' lives—bossy, domineering and always organising them. I produced little shows, making them sing, recite poetry and dance, and made costumes for them out of bits and pieces from Nanny's rag bag. I always visualised something exquisitely beautiful, but invariably felt disappointed as my productions never turned out as I wanted them.

I played a lot of tennis and, one year, succeeded in winning the Junior Tournament at the North Foreland Club. I was very proud of my prize—a pink enamel clock, which unfortunately, I overwound after only a few days.

The holidays were happy for me, marred only by the dread of returning to school. These feelings of nervous anticipation have plagued me all my life.

In 1935 we moved to Highgate, where we had a lovely garden with a hard tennis court. This proved a great attraction and we had plenty of social life. So far, my only experience of theatre-going had been an annual visit to the pantomime. Now, I often went out with my brothers and their friends to concerts, theatres and films.

The most memorable 'date' was with Ian, now a medical student at the London Hospital. He took me to the ballet at Sadlers' Wells and this outing changed my life.

It was the first time I had attended an evening performance. I wore my best navy-blue taffeta dress and long, white gloves. It was very hot and the theatre smelt of Turkish cigarettes; there was an air of suppressed excitement as we took our seats in the stalls. The orchestra started tuning up; Constant Lambert was conducting, and as he took his place on the rostrum amidst applause, the house lights dimmed. The curtain rose on *Les Sylphides*. The graceful, white-clad figures seemed to reflect the moonlight as they dreamily moved to

CHILDHOOD AND SCHOOLDAYS

the music of Chopin. It was a revelation to me. Such romantic beauty stirred my soul as never before. I was absolutely overwhelmed.

The rest of the programme was an anticlimax. It was the ballet blanc that converted me, and that night I decided to become a ballet dancer.

2

FIRST CAREER: THE BALLET

I was fourteen years old when I made this impetuous decision and it should have been obvious to me, a rather plump adolescent, that I was unsuited to the profession but my mind was made up. I would brook no interference and opposed any suggestions for an alternative career. In my ignorance, I saw myself in pink ballet shoes and a long white dress, floating around the stage in *Les Sylphides*. I had forgotten how arduous the ballet exercises had been and that it took a lifetime to perfect the technique that made those on stage appear so perfect. Those delicate-looking, ethereal dancers were very tough indeed, dedicated beings working for hours every day at classes, rehearsals and performances. Daily training throughout early childhood is vital to give any dancer sufficient strength and stamina for life in a ballet company. My once a week dancing classes would have been of some help but were definitely not enough. I had started about eight years too late, and however hard I worked now, I could never retrieve those lost years.

Very sensibly, my father insisted that I remain at school to take my school certificate, which I passed in the summer of 1939. In his opinion, I had not yet decided on a career, so he suggested that I should try to matriculate at Christmas.

During the summer holidays, however, war was declared, and when we returned to London, our school had been evacuated. Brighid, Alison and I were sent to the only school still functioning in Highgate. This was primarily a dancing school, and as the Principal was fully occupied with the physical training schedule for the Auxiliary Territorial

Service, we were taught by her students. We started work each morning at 8.30 and danced for two hours, learning the rudiments of Greek dancing and the Cecchetti method of ballet. Our general education was in the hands of two rather elderly governesses whom we fondly named 'Petty Bug' and 'Marrowbones'. There were only five of us in the class, so it wasn't surprising they got me through my matriculation that Christmas.

This was the period of the 'phoney war' and our lives carried on normally. The most exciting event was a garden party in aid of the Spitfire fund held in the grounds of one of the biggest houses in Highgate. Our school gave a dancing display during the afternoon in the rose garden. We had rehearsed hard for several weeks, but I felt very nervous as I got ready for the performance. It was not a very spectacular debut, but I was thrilled to be in costume and dancing to an audience at last.

I became a full-time student, determined to make the grade as a ballet dancer. I practised for hours in an empty room at the top of the house and read every book I could get hold of. This new world enchanted me and I became completely dedicated. I had made up my mind to go on the stage. My father was obviously very perturbed at this suggestion and had a serious talk with me about my future. He tried to dissuade me but I was adamant. Nothing else would satisfy me now.

My serious training was to be delayed by the bombing of London. Looking back on it now, we were lucky. Highgate was a comparatively safe area. Though we slept every night in the cellar, it was frightening. We could feel the house rocking overhead and hear the shriek of falling bombs. One night, our old house in Harley Street got a direct hit and was obliterated, the people in it killed. My father's consulting room in Queen Anne Street overlooked the pile of rubble that had once been our happy home. It was an appalling sight, and for the first time, the war seemed on our doorstep.

Father decided to send us out of London and sell the house. One of his patients lent us their bungalow in North Wales. This was situated half-way down a steep cliff with a magnificent view of Snowdonia across the bay; a beautiful place in summer, but we were to be there through a long cold winter. The bungalow was built of wood surrounded by a wide verandah, where Robin, Brighid, Alison and I did our daily exercises at the 'barre'. As a Christmas entertainment for our parents, we produced a ballet. Robin's choreography was ingenious and included some remarkable 'lifts'. There was no story but plenty of movement. Three 'celestial bodies', their heavenly brilliance portrayed in head-dresses made from metal milk bottle tops, encircled the 'Earth' adorned with ivy leaves and fir cones. We had no music whatever so it was a purely rhythmical performance, and our parents were delighted and most impressed.

Christmas this year was a very brief interlude and as soon as it was over, Father returned to London. He was running an Emergency Medical Centre there and, when he visited us, his only casualty to date had been a chap taking part in a Civil Defence exercise. The poor fellow's nose had been broken when a tin hat fell down on to his face as he was being carried on a stretcher to the hospital! I am afraid this caused immense amusement in our family.

As soon as there was a lull in the bombing, we returned to a house on the outskirts of London and I was able to start my career in earnest. My father still strongly disapproved of my decision to go on the stage, but advised me to obtain the best training available. Without hesitation, I wrote to Sadlers' Wells and asked for an audition. Within a few days, I received a letter from the Principal, Ursula Morton, asking me to appear the following week at a class. With only slight apprehension, I found my way to Islington and to the stage-

FIRST CAREER: THE BALLET

door of the Theatre. This had been badly blasted and most of the windows were boarded up with pieces of cardboard and wood. I groped my way through the darkness and climbed hundreds of stairs to the top of the building. The ballet room was in front of me, its windows intact; I was in daylight again and through the glass doors I could see a class already in progress.

Alongside was the dressing room full of people. Shyly, I changed into my white silk tunic tied at the waist with a red cord, white socks and red ballet shoes. This had been the uniform at my other dancing school and I was appalled to find everyone else in black tights and tunics looking most professional. Immediately I felt at a disadvantage.

I went into class and was introduced to Ursula Morton, a lovely, charming woman with dark expressive eyes and a calm, kind manner. Class started and I had the utmost difficulty keeping up with it. Obviously, these pupils were more advanced. I tried my best to copy them, floundering my way through and was nearly in tears by the end. Miss Morton realised that I was dreadfully nervous and tactfully suggested that I came twice a week to see how I progressed. I was thrilled and very relieved that she didn't turn me out and tell me not to come again.

In the dressing room afterwards, one of the girls suggested that I got myself the correct uniform. I was most grateful to her for this friendly advice and went home at once to see what could be achieved. Clothes were rationed and we had no coupons to spare for garments of this type. We had a pair of old black cotton tights in our dressing-up trunk which did service for many months, until I had gathered enough coupons for a pair of black woolly ones. I made myself a black silk tunic, and the next time I went to Sadlers' Wells I felt much less conspicuous in class.

On the days I did not go to London, I practised in the

garden. Conditions were far from ideal, but I felt that my technique was improving. I had never worked so hard in my life, but loved my days at the Wells. Classical ballet classes were given by either Ursula Morton or Nicholas Sergueff who had been regisseur at the Maryinsky Theatre in Leningrad. He was a wiry, bespectacled little man who always taught with a cane in his hand. He was not particularly careful where he tapped out the rhythm, and if he missed the barre and hit you by mistake it was just too bad! Ursula Morton took the National and Character dancing classes, in which we learnt excerpts from many ballets. These were most enjoyable and, amongst other things, I learnt to Mazurka correctly. This dance has a very subtle rhythm and is exceedingly difficult to master, but her thorough tuition was to play a significant part in my career.

After I had been at the school for a few weeks, Miss Morton sent for my mother. We were interviewed in her office and she told us that I was physically unsuited to be a member of the Company. This was a shattering blow to me and I was heart-broken. I would not accept my physical limitations. I had set my heart on the stage and still felt that, by working hard, my ambition could be achieved. Miss Morton obviously understood my disappointment and I was touched by her sympathy. To soften the blow, she suggested that I continued at the Wells twice a week. On the other days, I was to attend classes at the Cone School where I could take my dancing examinations and qualify as a teacher. The Cone sisters, Gracie, Lillie and Valerie, ran this flourishing school in the heart of London's West End. It was also a theatrical agency and pupils and students were often away working. We had to study all types of dancing; ballroom, tap, musical comedy and modern ballet. I hated it. I felt no enthusiasm at all for modern dancing and my sophisticated colleagues gave me an inferiority complex. To counteract this, I think I showed an unpleasant, superior attitude towards everyone and just lived for my days at the Wells.

Ursula Morton left and Ailne Phillips took her place. She had been a soloist in the company for several years but was a good teacher and achieved results in a quiet, decisive manner. We learnt many of the classical ballets; *Swan Lake, Les Sylphides, Sleeping Beauty* and excerpts from *Casse Noisette*. I begrudged the time I had to spend at the Cone School studying for my exams, but it had been a wise decision of Miss Morton's and it wasn't long before I realised that I would not have had the stamina to cope with life in a ballet company.

At the end of my first term at the Cone School, I took my Elementary examination for the Royal Academy of Dancing. Miss Gracie always took the final class which was also a dress rehearsal. Without consulting anyone, I had made what I thought was a regulation white ballet dress. At the end of the class, she took me into another room and told me that I could not possibly wear *that* dress for the examination! It had been made all wrong. She then explained the correct line and design of a tu-tu and lent me one of Dame Alicia Markova's old ones to copy. Material was still rationed and I don't think I made a very good job of remaking mine, but this second effort was passed.

I was surprised to find the examination a very nerve-wracking experience. The hall at the Royal Academy of Dancing was very large and I found it extremely difficult to hear the examiner's commands, which in ballet are always given in French. I only just scraped through and realised that I would have to work much harder in future.

The School moved to a large, beautiful house in Mayfair. Children swarmed back from the country, and as the numbers rapidly increased, the atmosphere changed and I began to enjoy my classes there. Within two years, I had completed my exams at the R.A.D., taken my Elementary and Intermediate Cecchetti, and Honours in my Greek dancing.

I left the Wells and became a student teacher at Cone's. In this capacity I would give classes in return for further training. I took the Solo Seal exam of the R.A.D., and, as usual before an examination, I became exceedingly nervous. As this final one drew near, I lost my voice. Dame Adeline Genée was one of the examiners and during the exam she asked me how I was feeling. I said I was very dry, and she replied in her delightful Danish accent, 'I'm so sorry, we are not allowed to serve drinks here!'

As soon as I knew I had passed successfully, my voice returned.

As a member of the Royal Academy of Dancing, I took part in several Production Club performances. In these, I danced in the corps de ballet with soloists from Sadlers' Wells. It was valuable experience and the acme of my dreams. I still longed to be a dancer.

Before long, the Cones took me on as a full-time member of their staff. Working hours were long and I was in the school from nine in the morning till seven at night. The knowledge I had acquired at the Wells' was tremendously useful and I was soon taking the National dancing classes throughout the school, teaching the seniors the Mazurka rhythm Miss Morton had so patiently instilled into me. Many talented pupils emerged from this school, names that are now famous in the theatre world; Julie Andrews, John Gilpin, Claire Bloom, Patricia Dainton and Natasha Parry, to name but a few.

I produced *Les Sylphides* for the junior ballet group and decided that it should be a full-scale production. The children helped me to make their costumes and they looked utterly charming. Unfortunately, the boy taking the male role was sent to an audition at the time of the performance. He had no under-study so there was no alternative but for me to dance in his place. I must say I felt a bit idiotic presenting the three soloists with the bouquets of flowers I had brought from the garden. The staff were very delighted with our efforts and I felt the work had all been worth while.

If I was going to be a successful teacher, it was essential for me to have some experience in the theatre and I decided to leave Cone's and go on the stage. My decision was unpopular but I think it was right. I simply had to get dancing out of my system before I settled down to teaching.

3

THE THEATRE

I STARTED taking classes from various well-known teachers, including Anna Sevenskaya, Vera Volkova, Stanislas Idzikovski, Lydia Kyasht and Lydia Sokolova. They taught in some studios in the heart of London's theatreland, and the dancers attending them were all professionals. It was at one of Anna Sevenskaya's classes that I heard there was to be an audition for a new member of the corps de ballet in *Song of Norway*.

This successful musical, based on the life and music of Edvard Greig, with choreography by Robert Helpmann and Pauline Grant, was running at the Palace Theatre. I went along there and found that I was one of about twelve girls trying for the vacancy. There was a lot of National and Character dancing in the show, so that the ballet master and leading dancer who took the audition asked us to show them some Mazurka steps. This was a lucky break for me and I was selected.

I changed my name to Elizabeth Scott, but this touch of professionalism was of little help as I went nervously round to meet the manager, and to sign the contract which gave me £6. 10s. a week. He was exceedingly kind, however, and suggested that I should watch a performance that evening.

The house was packed and I had to stand at the back of the stalls. I was entranced at the gaiety and high standard of the dancing, and thoroughly enjoyed the singing of Janet Hamilton Smith and John Hargreaves. I felt sure I was going to enjoy the work and looked forward to making my debut on the stage.

Solo Seal Examination for the Royal Academy of Dancing

A Penny Concert FOX PHOTOS

Pre-School Dancing Class KEYSTONE

THE THEATRE

The Company were very friendly and helpful. It isn't easy joining a show that has been running for several months, and I had to learn my part within a week with only one morning's rehearsal with the rest of the corps de ballet. My first night was nerve-wracking, but with a little prompting from my colleagues, I somehow managed to struggle through it. My only faux pas was a late entry in the last ballet when I almost collided with Moira Fraser, the 'Spirit of Norway'. I apologised to her after the show and she was most kind and told me not to worry. But of course I did, and was nervous about this part of the ballet for weeks to come.

Regular classes, rehearsals and eight shows a week—I felt I was a professional at last. It was thrilling to go through the stage door and up to the dressing room, with its haunting smell of grease paint and atmosphere of suppressed excitement. This was the life I had wanted.

When I had been in the show a few months, I was asked by one of the leading dancers if I would like to join him and another girl and take a ballet act to the Butlin's Holiday Camps. There were only three in existence then and we were to give two shows on Sunday evenings at each of them. It sounded an interesting proposition, as we were to be the first ballet seen there. I accepted with alacrity and started rehearsing.

Our act consisted of duets, solos and a Mazurka pas de trois. We had lovely costumes and set off with great enthusiasm for our first performance at Clacton. We arrived on a Sunday afternoon in time to try out the minute stage. All we had heard about the camps was true; cheerful, red-coated workers greeted us on our arrival. The loudspeakers proclaimed that we were just in time for the 'knobbly knees' competition. Everyone was made to feel young and jolly; 'Lads' and 'Lassies' on the doors instead of 'Ladies' and 'Gentlemen'; happy campers everywhere; a 'Hi de hi' and a

'Ho de ho!'. Our performances went down well and we retired to chalets for the night.

Early next morning, the loudspeakers were requesting campers to get up for their early morning exercises. We left the camp immediately after breakfast, utterly exhausted.

A week later I developed measles and was out of *Song of Norway* for three weeks. I had never felt so ill in my life. My temperature soared and I thought I was going to die. I was frightened. I didn't want to die. Life was too good. I prayed for recovery and vowed that, if this was granted, I would do something to help others. I had time to reflect, and concluded that I was being rather selfish and self-centred.

As soon as I was convalescent, I tried out my part in the show. My mind was a complete blank and I could not remember a single step! For a moment I panicked, but as I concentrated hard on the music, it all gradually came back to me. By the time I went back to the theatre and had a run-through in the dressing room, all was well. I was delighted to be back and got a great welcome from the Company.

I had missed the performances at the other Butlin Camps, but danced at their reunion at the Albert Hall. It was a very strange sensation pirouetting alone in that vast arena. The audience and spotlights were all around and there seemed to be no focal point. Our performance seemed to go well and, judging by the applause, we were very popular.

Auditions for *Annie Get Your Gun* were being held at the Coliseum when *Song of Norway* ended. I was tired and felt in need of a holiday, so I didn't think in terms of another show. This decision put me out of work for several months and I learnt a valuable lesson. When working in the theatre, never think of having a holiday or you may find yourself with a prolonged one!

During this interval, I did some television and some filming, but I missed the contact with a live audience. With the approach of Christmas, however, work was plentiful and I auditioned successfully for the first big pantomime held at the Palladium since the war. Austerity was forgotten, and the costumes were superb. There was a wonderful cast headed by Tommy Trinder, Evelyn Laye and the Bernard Brothers. The Palladium is an ideal theatre from an artiste's point of view and I thoroughly enjoyed the three months I worked there.

Not long after this was over, I started rehearsing a new Ivor Novello show, *King's Rhapsody*, a musical play with book and lyrics by Christopher Hassall. Choreography was by Pauline Grant, who had also produced the dances in the Pantomime. We opened at the Palace Theatre, Manchester, where I had my first and last experience of theatrical digs. I am afraid I was not cut out for the rigours of touring, but it did make me appreciate the comforts of home. In spite of early morning calls and all-night rehearsals, I enjoyed the preparation and creation of this beautiful show.

King's Rhapsody was an immediate success, and within three months of opening in London we had covered production costs, which were around the £60,000 mark. Costumes were gorgeous and exquisitely made, an extravaganza and riot of colour. My costume for the ballroom scene cost £200, and was made of the loveliest French silk in delicate shades of pink and grey, and trimmed with silver and white.

After three weeks in Manchester, we moved back to the Palace Theatre, London, where we stayed until the show came off in 1951.

This was a happy show with a very united cast. Ivor Novello was a unique person, kind and generous to all who worked with him. His hospitality was lavish and every anniversary was an excuse for a party. Outings were numerous, and sometimes the company were entertained in his home. His lovely house was filled with treasures and I was amazed that his valuable Jade collection was left lying around for our inspection. His swimming pool, tennis court, croquet lawn and beautiful grounds were at our disposal and we were free to wander wherever we wished. Novello always said he enjoyed himself a hundred times more if he had a hundred people with him. He was notably kind and thoughtful when he heard that my brother had to undergo a serious operation. He offered him the use of his extensive library and each week new laid eggs, still very scarce, were delivered to my dressing room. I thought this generosity most touching.

Twice during the run of *King's Rhapsody*, the theatre closed and we had a week's holiday, partly at Novello's expense. The first time, I went to Paris with a friend from the Ballet Rambert and attended classes given by Olga Preobrajenskaya. She was petite and charming, and in spite of advancing years, had quick, bird-like movements. She used to sprinkle the floor with a tiny watering-can. She gave lovely classes and was extremely kind to the 'English girls'.

We were doing eight shows a week and an occasional midnight charity matinée, but I still felt that theatre life was rather empty. I was put in touch with the organizing secretary of Coram's Fields. This playground is in the heart of Bloomsbury on the site of the original foundling Hospital, started by Captain Coram for destitute and unwanted children. The grounds are lovely and the tennis courts, football pitches and paddling pool are much used by the children living in this crowded area of London. There are several large halls in the grounds which are used for Scouts and Guides meetings and classes of various kinds.

The Management Committee were planning pre-school classes on two afternoons a week. These were intended to wean children under five gently from their parents in preparation for school. I was asked if I would teach the group dancing and musical movement, while a Froebel-trained teacher taught them painting and handwork. So that no child should be excluded, the total cost for an hour's lesson was 6d. Parents quickly recognised that this was good value. Knowledge of them spread quickly round the district and a steady stream of children filled them for several years.

I taught in the Band room where Handel had rehearsed the famous Foundling choir. The first class was difficult. I was faced with approximately thirty small, nameless children and a lot of worried mothers. I memorised a few names, but the others were 'You with the pigtails' 'You with the red shoes' or 'The boy with the green tie', and so on. If they were tearful, I let the mothers stay, but most of them settled down after a few classes and were happy to remain with me on their own.

After I had been taking the pre-school group for a short time, I was asked if I would organise a dancing section to be included in the 'Penny Concerts'. These were held in the Band room on Saturday mornings and cost, as the name suggests, one penny, for which the children received a printed programme. The artistes taking part were professionals and accepted only expenses by way of payment. Violet Graham organized the musical section and she usually had two or three other musicians to play with her. I organised the dancing section, partnered by someone from 'King's Rhapsody' or one of the other West End shows. The musicians accompanied us and we all took great pride in trying to produce a high standard of entertainment for the children.

We gave seven concerts during the winter months, one concert per month. They were popular, not only with the children, but with their parents and schools, and were always very well attended. Without being boastful, I think they were marvellous value for money.

At the start of each season, Violet and I discussed the series as a whole. We tried to link them comprehensively, preceding each item with a short explanation. The concerts were primarily for the children's enjoyment, but we also tried to give them a little knowledge of the origin and history of the works performed. Much of the dancing was specially choreographed to appeal to the children, but we also gave them National, Character and Historical dances, excerpts from the Classical ballets and a demonstration ballet class.

The Christmas concert was always a *pièce de résistance*. One year, with the help of nine musicians, we produced *Peter and the Wolf*. This was woven into a fairy tale about a doll on the Christmas tree coming to life, and drew an audience of five hundred.

The rehearsing of these dances took up a lot of time; they were often fitted in during the intervals of the Show, backstage, on the roof, in the corridor—anywhere where there was space to move. Pianists were costly and rehearsals with them had to be kept to a minimum. I made many of the costumes myself until Ivor Novello heard of my work and asked a theatrical costumier to lend us some free of charge.

In one corner of Coram's Fields, there was an open air school run by the London County Council. The Headmistress, after seeing my work with the pre-school groups and at the 'Penny Concerts', asked me if I would be interested in taking classes there once a week. After lengthy discussions at County Hall, permission was granted and I took three classes on Wednesday mornings—Matinée day!

The lessons had to be specially adapted, as the children attending this school were delicate and many of them had breathing difficulties. For this reason, we worked with doors and windows wide open. This was good for us all and we were always starving by the end of the morning.

To celebrate the school's birthday, eight of my colleagues from *King's Rhapsody* joined me in presenting a morning of ballet for the children. Some of the dances were specially composed for the occasion and the programme included some of the favourite numbers from the 'Penny Concerts' and some excerpts from the Classical ballets. We spent hours rehearsing it and begged, borrowed or made the costumes. The show was followed by a festive luncheon party with the children and it was a rather weary troupe that returned to the Palace Theatre in time for the Matinée.

Novello's sudden death was a shock to everyone. When the curtain rang down the night before, he had said 'goodnight' to us as usual. It seemed incredible that it had been his last appearance. There was no show that evening and the Matinée the following day was one of the saddest performances imaginable. It was a terrible strain for all of us. The show ran for a few months longer but was never quite the same again. When it ended, I decided to give up the Theatre. Though I loved it, I realised that real enjoyment in my work lay in teaching.

I had had six years on stage and the experience had been invaluable. I had lost much of my timidity but never succeeded in conquering my nervousness. I was far too sensitive and soft to cope with the toughness of show business, but I would not have missed these years for anything.

. . . . .

I had one more show to do—the Ivor Novello Memorial Show. Stars from every aspect of the theatre, including such great names as Kirsten Flagstaed, Noel Coward, Emlyn Williams, Gracie Fields and many others, made this an unforgettable evening at the Coliseum. The show opened with the ballet dancing to a selection of waltzes from Novello's many successful shows. Dressed in Empire-style pink chiffon dresses, our partners in blue and gold military uniforms, we set the tone for a romantic and memorable evening. I was proud to have taken part in this tribute to a versatile and great artist.

4

POLIO STRIKES

NINETEEN-FIFTY-THREE, the year the whole pattern of my life was to change. It started with my father's retirement to a remote village in Kent, where he hoped for peace and quiet in which to write. His final year had been a hectic one. Great Ormond Street was celebrating its centenary, and to commemorate this event he had written a short history of the hospital. Two specially bound copies were inscribed and presented by my father—one to the Queen and the other to Princess Royal, then Patroness of the hospital.

As part of these celebrations, I was asked to produce a ballet for a children's party. It was for all ex-patients and held under a marquee in the courtyard of the hospital. A large stage was built at one end of this and the children from the wards were wheeled out on to the balconies for a grandstand view of the proceedings. Two excellent clowns entertained them and about twenty of my pupils danced a short '1852 Ballet'.

I had spent some time in the print room of the Victoria and Albert Museum, searching for authentic designs for the costumes and every day, the children rehearsed hard after school. Some of the mothers helped me to make the dresses and the result was worth all the effort. It seemed a pity we were to give only a single performance. I therefore arranged to show it at some old people's clubs and schools for handicapped children.

After the performance at the Mary Ward School, the Headmistress asked me if I had any free time, as she desperately needed a kindergarten teacher. Although I was unqualified, I agreed to help. I had always had a horror of illness and disfigurement and had to steel myself to face these pathetic little people. Their maimed and crippled bodies appalled me and my heart ached for them. It was always a relief to get back to my dancing classes. The first few days were a terrible strain, but I gradually got used to it and remained there until after Christmas when the new kindergarten teacher arrived.

When my father retired, Robin and I moved to the Chelsea Studios. These had been built by an Italian sculptor who felt there was a great need for suitable studios for artists in London. Behind an eight-foot wall, he created an Italian village. Tiles and wrought iron, vines and small sculptures gave this unique site a continental atmosphere. When we arrived, the walls of our new home were hidden under clusters of brilliant yellow laburnum flowers and, as the summer progressed, this gave way to a profusion of wisteria and sweet-smelling jasmine. It crept in at the windows and made us forget we were in the heart of London—a London that was crowded with people who had come to this country for the Coronation of Queen Elizabeth II, a London that was thrilled with the tremendous news of the conquest of Everest. Life was full of excitement and promise.

My time was fully occupied with teaching and running the flat, but one day the principal teacher at the Royal School of Needlework, who knew of my interest in sewing, asked me if I would like to help at the forthcoming exhibition of the Royal Coronation robes. This was to be held at St. James' Palace and it sounded fascinating. I gladly accepted.

The exhibition started the week following the Coronation and included many of the Royal robes, Orders and Regalia. I was one of about a dozen helpers constantly guarded by the C.I.D., and we worked in two shifts—10 a.m. to 4 p.m., and 4 p.m. to 10 p.m. Every robe had its own calico cover which was put on each night. The morning shift uncovered them and gently removed any trace of dust with tiny vacuum cleaners. We sold catalogues, embroidery outfits and small souvenirs of the specially woven purple velvet of the Coronation robe and tried to answer numerous questions put to us by the public. Needless to say, there was always somebody available to whom we could turn for correct answers.

The opening night was televised, with a commentary by Richard Dimbleby. It was opened by Queen Elizabeth the Queen Mother, accompanied by the Duke and Duchess of Gloucester and Princess Royal. It was very colourful and the Queen Mother was wearing a tiara and shimmering crinoline. She looked superb, and I was thrilled and delighted when she shook my hand.

My days seemed very hectic, rushing between teaching, the Palace, the flat, always on the go.

The exhibition had been running for three weeks when, one evening, my sister Janet telephoned me to say that her three-months-old baby, John, had been rushed into Great Ormond Street with suspected meningitis. As she was breast-feeding him, she was admitted too and I went to look after her other son, Nicholas, then about eighteen months old.

John became desperately ill and one evening, Janet came back saying she did not expect him to live through the night. Feeling heart-broken, I went back to the flat. When the 'phone rang early the following morning to say that John was still alive, I could hardly believe it. Could I go back and take charge of Nicholas again? This I did willingly, as Janet's place was obviously with John.

During the next few days, Nicholas became very fretful and I thought he was missing his mother. I cuddled and comforted him as best I could, but he seemed inconsolable. It was not until later that we realised he too was ill.

POLIO STRIKES

I had to miss my duties at the Palace, but continued whenever possible to take my dancing classes.

John's crisis was past and he was definitely on the mend when Janet was taken ill, also with suspected meningitis. She was admitted into the National Hospital, Queen Square, which practically adjoins Great Ormond Street. I took Nicholas to his grandparents, Dr. and Mrs. Trounce, which left me free to go back to my work.

On a hot July morning, I set off to take my usual Saturday classes in Bloomsbury. I felt unwell and bought a thermometer on the way. I took my temperature and, to my horror, found it was 102°! At the end of the morning, I realised I needed professional advice and walked round to Great Ormond Street to consult my brother-in-law, David, who was a doctor there. I hadn't bothered to register with a general practitioner, as I never expected to be ill! He told me to go home and if I was still running a temperature to let him know. When I got back to the flat, I felt very light-headed and discovered my temperature was even higher. David came over and examined me, but the only thing he found wrong was slight pharyngitis. Both Robin and I were to be away that weekend so there was no food in the flat. David gave me some tablets and told me to go to Kent as planned if my temperature was normal on the following morning. It was, so off I went.

My father met me off the train and we drove down to the beach and had a look at the sea. It was lovely after the nightmare, rush and worry of the past two weeks. In the afternoon we lazed in the garden in the sun. I didn't feel too bad, just lethargic and very tired. Monday morning came and I still felt desperately tired and slightly off-colour, so I decided to take another day off. I thought it was just reaction but, in the afternoon when I took the dog for a walk across the fields, I noticed that I got a sharp pain over my head and a stiffness at the back of my neck whenever I looked down. Then I knew that I really was ill and went to bed as soon as I got home.

The following morning, my parents called in their doctor, a tall, white-haired, kindly man, his face readily crinkling into laughter. Dr. Boulden, though I didn't know it at the time, was to become a wonderful friend. He examined me, returning again at lunch time to perform a lumbar puncture. This was a most unpleasant experience, but later, I discovered that my reaction to it was unusual. I felt the complete outline of my nervous system. It was like an electric shock. My hands became like claws and I went into a kind of spasm. This quickly passed off. The results confirmed that there was something seriously wrong and I must be admitted into hospital right away. The nearest bed available was in Eastbourne, so it was arranged that I should join Janet in the National.

My mother came with me in the ambulance and it took us four hours to reach London. During the journey, the same clawlike sensations returned to my hands, but as I did not feel very ill, I was able to direct the driver to the entrance to Queen Square which is very hard to find. The hospital is on the opposite side of the square to the hall where I held my classes. These were taking place at that very moment, my pianist deputising for me, and I hoped that none of my pupils would see me.

I was wheeled on a trolley into the ward and put into a bed beside my sister. This was my first experience of being a patient in hospital and it was comforting to find Janet next to me. We were curtained off together as we might be infectious. Just how infectious and what was wrong with us no-one seemed to know.

Strange noises reached us in our secluded corner which gave me an extraordinary impression of the workings of a hospital ward. One clear memory I have is of a doctor's conversation with one of the patients. He was putting her through the standard neurological tests. 'Put out your tongue.' Silence. . . 'Screw up your eyes.' Again silence. . . Then, 'Show me your teeth.' 'They're on the locker, doctor!'

I was also subjected to these tests and performed them all successfully. My cheerful frame of mind rather misled the doctors.

I do not remember my legs becoming paralysed, but on Wednesday morning, I was aware that I could not move my left arm. I also had the utmost difficult in reaching the drinking water from my locker. My arms felt so wobbly that I kept spilling it. When I flopped back on the bed exhausted by the exertion, Janet would hop out of her bed to help me. However, I was cheerful and alert, taking an interest in the happenings of the ward both on the far side of the screen and in our little corner.

John was brought round twice a day for Janet to feed and I remember talking to a doctor from Great Ormond Street who asked me how I was feeling. When I told him I could not move my left arm, he did not seem unduly worried so I did not worry either.

On Thursday morning, however, I found I couldn't breathe normally. I could only manage half breaths. The nurse came as soon as I called and suddenly, it flashed across my mind what was wrong with me. 'I've got polio, haven't I?' Then, perhaps dramatically, added, 'I'll never dance again!'

Nurse was Scottish, and her reply was terse and to the point.

'You're going to be worse before you're better!'

Suddenly, my bed was surrounded by people and I was wheeled out of the ward. I looked back at Janet. I hope I shall never see that expression on her face again. She looked stricken.

No-one told me where I was going and the journey seemed endless; along corridors, up lifts, along more corridors and eventually into a room which seemed full of people in white gowns and masks. I realised I was going to be put into an iron lung.

Long ago, Nanny had shown me a photograph of the very first iron lung and conjured up in my imagination a vivid picture of how it worked. As a small child, I had a sickening vision of a patient's head being squeezed through a tight rubber collar and I thought I was going to have to face this horrifying ordeal. Great was my relief when I saw them unclip a press-stud and fit it round my neck without any problems at all.

By this time I was gasping and very apprehensive, but the staff were working fast and it wasn't long before they pushed me in, clamped down the front of the lung and switched on the motor. I could breathe again.

Immediately, I thought I was well. I thought I would be in this machine for only a few hours. How little I knew! By the time I was taken out that evening, I could not breathe at all. I was completely paralysed from the neck down.

5

IN THE IRON LUNG

LOOKING back on those early days, my memory is perhaps blurred in places, but some events and feelings are still startlingly clear. Although I did not know at the time, I was desperately ill and fought instinctively to live. Doctors and nurses worked with grim determination. The engineers kept constant watch outside my room in case anything went wrong with the iron lung.

I had the luck to be in the one hospital in the world where a positive pressure machine was in the process of being invented. This was the Beaverometer, named after the inventor, Dr. Beaver, senior anaesthetist at the National Hospital. His machine was used to keep me breathing while I came out of the lung for washing, medical attention and later, physiotherapy. Although there was always an anaesthetist holding my mask and regulating the pressure, I suffered agonies of fear and was terrified of suffocating. The action of the Beaverometer was quite different from that of the iron lung. A mask covered my face and air was forcibly pushed into my lungs, whereas the action of the lung seemed much gentler and I was less conscious of being machine-breathed.

So far, the Beaverometer had only been used on unconscious patients. The first time the mask was clamped on to my face and the iron lung switched off, I could not understand what was happening. The machine did not seem to be breathing me. I shook my head to indicate this to the doctor, and it wasn't until Dr. Beaver came and explained the difference between the action of the two machines that I was able to co-operate.

Everyone entering my room wore masks and gowns and I was not always aware of identities. I got used to the weird, remote, antiseptic atmosphere which had rather a theatrical air about it. If I had not felt so ill and exhausted, I might have enjoyed the quality of the performance—it was so polished and professional. Lying flat on my back, night and day, with only my head outside my machine surrounded by these masked figures, I became very conscious of the beauty of people's eyes. If the saying is true that 'the eyes are the mirror of the soul', then I was being cared for by Saints.

This was my first experience of severe illness and there was nothing about it that appealed to me. I loathed the lack of privacy, and degrading treatments to which my body was subjected under the eyes of doctors and nurses and in the presence of mechanics. All my nursing care, medical treatment and any attention needed by the iron lung had to be completed as quickly as possible whilst I was out on the Beaverometer, so these sessions were always rather public affairs. Every six hours, my team descended on me and I was faced with the nightmare of leaving the iron lung. Day after day, I had to fight down feelings of panic and fear and was utterly exhausted by it all. Very occasionally, something went wrong with the machines. Everything went black and I lost touch with the world. Within seconds I was back in the lung, gasping and shivering with fright.

Sleep was elusive. My mind seemed to work continuously. I was haunted by imaginary music which never ceased, and saw endless shapes and figures, vividly coloured, moving and revolving before my eyes. My head throbbed and ached and my whole body felt cramped and horribly deformed. The clanking of the iron lung motor resolved, in my imagination, into the engines of a ship and I thought I was at sea. Drugs made me say stupid things. I knew they were silly but could not be bothered to make myself in-

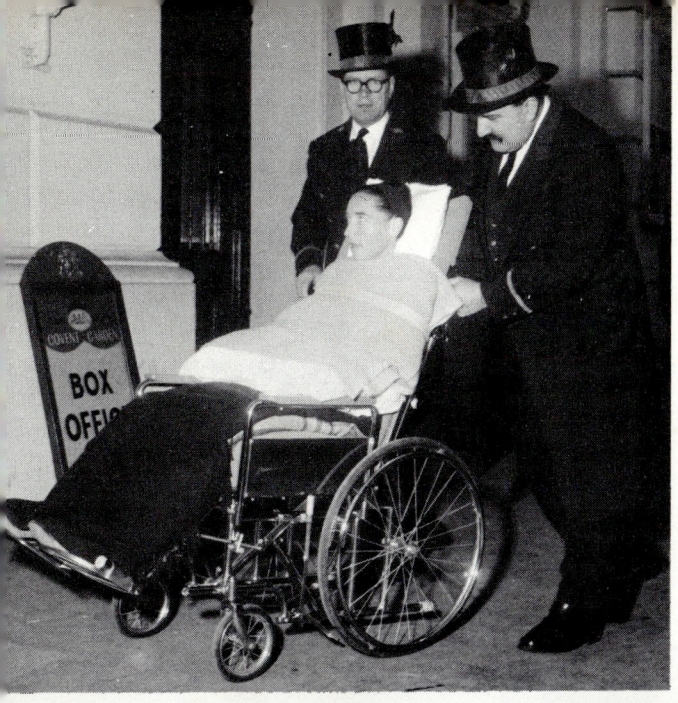

Arriving at Covent Garden

KEYSTONE

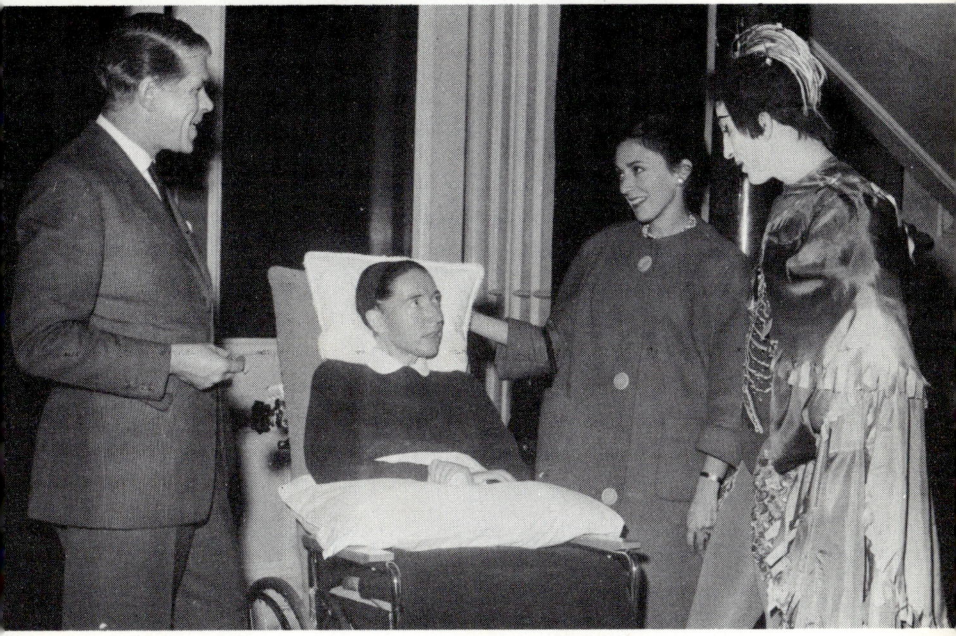

After the performance talking to Annette Page, Ronald Hynd and Mr. Beresford **KEYSTONE**

In a box at the Royal Opera House KEYSTONE

telligible. I lay idle, unable to rouse myself to take an interest in anything that was going on. The nurse specialling me tried reading, but it irritated and tired me. My parents, who were living in the hospital, made brief visits, but talking to them against the machine was exhausting and I was always glad when they went away.

During my fifth week in the lung, Dr. Gilliat became Resident Medical Officer. He was a tall, dark, good-looking man who took life very seriously. It was three weeks before I got a smile out of him, but as I came to know him better, I discovered beneath this solemn façade a charming, sensitive person, completely dedicated to his work.

His first words to me were, 'What are your interests in life, young lady?' I was usually asked, 'And how are we today?' Here was somebody different. I was shaken out of myself. By the end of the day he had organised a record player and a steady supply of records for me from the local public library. He was quick to understand my fear of suffocating and took immediate steps to prevent further mishaps with the machines. He insisted on having two Beaverometers and a double supply of oxygen permanently beside the lung, which meant that if one machine broke down, it was only a matter of switching over to the other. There would be no undue delay and this went a long way towards easing my mind.

He spent hours making further improvements to the Beaverometer—with Dr. Beaver's sanction of course; he wanted to make the face mask 'nurse-proof' (his words!) In fact, he changed the mask for an aqualung mouthpiece which I used with a nose-clip. This made it easy for a nurse to hold in place, and released the services of the anaesthetist.

In spite of my illness, I was very aware that I was being a useful 'guinea pig'. I was able to tell the doctors exactly how it felt to be on the receiving end of this new invention.

These improvements took months to perfect and, in spite

of nursing sessions, physiotherapy and musical interludes, time seemed to stand still. But it didn't. Days slipped by into weeks and weeks into months, but there was still no sign of movement in any part of my body.

During those early months in hospital, I was too ill to visualise what life held in store and it was some time before I realised that I was going to be paralysed for the rest of my life. This grim fact gradually penetrated my mind and, when it did, I felt utterly devastated. I gave way to black despair and hopeless depression. When I awoke each morning and found myself still entombed in my iron lung, I saw no end to my predicament and had little desire to live. I did not want to be a helpless, useless lump of humanity, dependent on others for every tiny movement and act of living. I had been a dancer with control over my body. Mentally, I still had this power, but there was no physical response. How could I face a life of complete immobility?

Every minute of the day and night, machines kept me breathing and there seemed no prospect of release. There was to be no escape for me for many months.

The first thing I *had* to do was learn to breathe on my own. Now and again, Dr. Gilliat would come in with a stopwatch, switch off the machine and tell me to breathe. It was hopeless. I was like a fish on dry land. Within seconds I was navyblue. It took three months to do a minute and a half on my own, and after seven months, I managed a quarter of an hour. My progress was so slow that it seemed negligible.

I did progress though, in spite of everything, and watched the seasons changing in the square below. Queen Square is a quiet oasis, protected from the noise of Southampton Row and Guilford Street by the surrounding buildings. On two sides there are hospitals, and on fine days the patients came out on to the lawns. Elderly inhabitants of Bloomsbury sat on the benches under the shady trees feeding the pigeons and sometimes in the evening, white habited nuns from the Italian Hospital took the air. All this I could see in an adjustable mirror attached to the front of my iron lung. I lived in a kind of mirror world, watching the on-goings in the square below, the birds feeding on the verandah behind my head, and the television—the screen of which had been reversed so that I saw it the right way round and everyone else saw it mirror-wise. Some of the doctors came to watch the boat race and got so muddled as to which crew was which, they left in disgust to watch the rest of the race on an unadulterated set.

I had been in the lung a year when I had a very severe set-back. I developed a kidney stone which made me seriously ill again for a few weeks. Drips, drugs, injections and nasal feeds—I felt I was back to square one. Fortunately for me, the stone was dispersed medically and I was saved the ordeal of a surgical operation.

One morning, I caught a glimpse of myself in the mirror and realised I looked as ghastly as I felt. My face was a revolting putty-grey. The mirror was promptly removed by the nurse. On my worst day, Matron walked in carrying a bunch of beautiful pink and blue sweetpeas. They were from the Duke of Kent. He had been involved in a car crash and was a patient in the room immediately above mine. He had been told about me and thought I would like the flowers. I hope Matron conveyed my thanks. I felt too ill to do this adequately.

This crisis passed and I resumed my twice daily sessions with the physiotherapist—passive movements and artificial respiration to strengthen my breathing muscles. She used to count the number of breaths I could achieve, and on the day we reached a hundred, there was great rejoicing and we were both purple in the face with the exertion. Soon, I was lifted on to a bed for part of the day. This was sometimes slightly raised and I saw, for the first time since my illness, complete people. It was a revelation! I had not realised how much I judged a person by the way they moved.

My physiotherapist now had more scope. She worked hard to find some movement in my body but alas, this was almost negligible. What little movement I had was in my neck and right arm. She suspended my arm in a sling from a beam which had been erected over my bed and I was able to swing it to and fro. After a few months of this I felt exasperated and longed to put the movement to some practical use. Every exercise in a ballet class has a purpose and leads on to something more difficult, and I felt my physiotherapy should have a similar motive.

An outstanding personality at the hospital was Sheridan Russell, one of the Almoners. Of Spanish origin, this lively, brilliant man was always bubbling over with original ideas. He had a tremendous sense of fun and was exceedingly sensitive to the feelings of others. He spoke five languages fluently, and before he took up welfare work, had been a professional cellist of outstanding merit. He suggested that I might be able to use an electric typewriter and somehow persuaded the Westminister Bank to give me one of their old ones to try. The prospect of doing something constructive was exhilarating, but oh, it was so much harder than I had anticipated! I found it impossible to breathe and type at the same time. I could do one or the other but simply could *not* do both together. It took years of practice before I could type with any degree of accuracy and speed. Serveral times a week, Sheridan would send me little notes written on the back of E.E.G. paper—often only a couple of witty or amusing lines. My first effort at a letter in reply was not very successful. The first one was 'DEAF M? BUSSELL'. The second one, 'DEAD MTRUSSELL'. I think he felt they almost equalled his letters for humour, even though the errors were accidental.

I did not realise the uniqueness of the National Hospital until I left eighteen months later. There was always a very relaxed, peaceful atmosphere about the place with an easy, gentle routine. Everyone was phenomenally kind and went out of their way to make me feel as happy as circumstances permitted. During the preliminary weeks of crises, my only visitors were my parents, the immediate hospital staff, and my sister Janet, who was still a patient there.

As I recovered and felt more sociable, visitors were permitted whenever it was convenient and I was rarely alone for long. All kinds of things took place there that would not have been tolerated in other hospitals. Family, friends, the hospital staff, and often complete strangers, popped in to help, cheer, or just chat. I knew most of the hospital gossip and was often a kind of communications centre, passing and receiving messages. People would dash in and ask, 'Where's Doctor So and-so?' or, 'Did you see where Miss Thingummy went?' Funnily enough, I was often able to tell them!

My room was sometimes a place of entertainment. Matron would sing amusing songs for me, accompanying the performance with appropriate actions. Two of her favourites were 'Count your Blessings' and 'There was an old Woman'. She has a chuckling sense of humour, a deep understanding of people and a tremendous desire to help solve the almost insurmountable problems that face so many of her patients. She always seems to have plenty of time to listen, effusing an aura of peace and tranquillity around her, which is truly a great gift. On my blackest days when she found me in floods of tears, she would indicate the sherry bottle on my locker and say, 'Have a little of Matron's medicine dear. It'll do you good.'

Once, Sheridan gave me a lunch hour recital of unaccompanied Bach on his cello, presenting *me* with a bouquet at the end of the performance! One of the nurses tried out her audition aria for an opera company one day, and another time, an African nurse demonstrated the rhumba! Occasionally, Sister suggested a little less noise and hilarity, but these performances did much to make life pleasanter for me.

I had a never-ending stream of visitors and I am still amazed at the kindness and constancy of these people. I felt sorry for them too. They must all have felt shocked and overwhelmed at what had happened, but none of them ever showed me their feelings. They were wonderful. Their encouragement and cheerfulness were exactly what I needed and because of them I was later able to face the outside world.

Until I could type my own letters, my family were kept very busy acknowledging presents. I was never without flowers during my entire stay at the National. Some of the gifts remain outstanding in my memory because they were so unexpected. The bouquets from Dame Margot Fonteyn on the eve of her wedding brought to me by two of the boys from the Royal Ballet; flowers from my little pupils; a lovely bunch of yellow roses from the Royal School of Needlework, and a present from Dame Adeline Genée, President of the Royal Academy of Dancing. Dame Adeline approached the porter and asked if she could see 'little Miss Higgins'. He peered over his glasses and said, 'She's quite a big girl now, Madame!'

She was so sweet and I was delighted to make her acquaintance other than in the examination hall, but still felt slightly awed in her presence.

I had some unexpected visitors too. I was thrilled to meet two members of the successful Everest team, Dr. Griffith Pugh and Tom Bourdillon. The breathing difficulties they faced to reach the summit were the exact opposite of mine at sea level. I had plenty of air and no muscles: they had marvellous physiques but hardly any air. Survival for all of us depended on mechanical assistance and they were extremely interested in my equipment.

All these gestures were most touching and remain happy memories shining through months of anguish.

My progress, however slight, was always a cause for celebration. My first outing into Queen Square, which I knew so intimately mirror-wise, was quite a procession. One warm Sunday morning when the square was very quiet, I went out on a trolley accompanied by two nurses, a doctor and a physiotherapist. It was the first time I had left the hospital building, but with such an entourage, I had little fear of leaving my machines. There seemed to be people at every window waving to me (which was rather embarrassing) and it was strange to be looking up at the hospital where they had saved my life.

One of my best companions was Jenny Poynting, my night special. We had many common interests and got on so well together that Matron 'forgot' to take her off night duty, and she looked after me for over a year. She was an excellent nurse and took a great interest in my progress. Now that I had braved the outside world, she often came back after breakfast to take me out. The trolley was discarded and an old wicker spinal carriage with a black mackintosh hood was produced from the depths of the hospital. One doctor said that Florence Nightingale had brought it back with her from the Crimea! I simply hated this vehicle but it was my only means of transport and I had to use it for my first social engagement.

I was invited to Coram's Fields for the opening of the new Band room by Lady Cynthia Colville. I was very apprehensive, and at lunch time, told my doctor I did not think I could face it. Jenny and another nurse persuaded me to go and, unknown to me, had arranged for Ken, one of my ex-dancing partners, to come and push me. They put some make-up on my face, tucked me into my vehicle and placed a Beaverometer under my feet for use in emergencies. The 'pram' tended to veer off the pavement and my escorts had difficulty manoeuvring it. Ken was a born clown and made the most of it. By the time we arrived, we were all slightly hysterical.

Lord Esher greeted me and presented me with a bouquet. I had to face quite a crowd, including press photographers and some of my little pupils, but the outing was not the ordeal I had anticipated. One amusing incident occurred; someone was worried that I might be getting breathless. To reassure her I said, 'Don't worry, I have a breathing machine under my feet.' 'Oh!' she said, 'I didn't know they could breathe you that way nowadays!'

Eventually, the sad day came when I had to leave the National. I was given a tremendous send-off. Sheridan produced a little red carpet over which I was wheeled. Matron, sisters, doctors and nurses—in fact, the whole hospital it seemed to me, found time to wave me on my way. I was packed, with utmost care, into a waiting ambulance. A nurse and a doctor accompanied me with precious breathing equipment. Suddenly, CRASH! The ambulance door disappeared. A motorist, distracted by all the excitement, had knocked it off!

· · · · ·

My destination was the Royal National Orthopaedic Hospital at Stanmore. I was miserable at leaving Queen Square where they had saved my life and nursed me with such loving care, and I felt sick with apprehension as I thought of my future in a completely new environment surrounded by strangers. Fortunately, the journey was short, as it was my first time on the road for over eighteen months. As we turned the corner into Guilford Street, one of the Beaverometers crashed to the floor. The journey was certainly proving eventful!

It was a cold, dark February day, and as we drove through the iron gates at Stanmore, the place looked bleak and inhospitable. After a considerable delay at the Administrative Block, we made our way towards the wards. These were mostly old Army huts set either side of a concrete covered way. The rest of the hospital consisted of many single-storied buildings scattered around acres of ground. There was a further delay while they fetched a trolley, then I was pushed into Hut 8. This was a vast, high-ceilinged room, with windows and French doors on three sides, making it light and very airy. There were twenty beds, and it struck me as being sterile—stark and unhomely. A Naval Commander who visited me later remarked,

'If Heaven is as clean as this, I hope I go to the other place!'

The iron lung was just inside the door. I soon realised that the orthopaedic staff on duty had had little or no experience of respirators. My apprehension increased. The doctor and nurse who had brought me put me into the machine, set the dials to the correct pressure and left.

I felt utterly miserable, homesick and lonely. But, obviously, I could *never* be alone here. Placed as I was, just inside the door, people were constantly passing me to and fro. I felt vulnerable and very exposed. Already I was missing the seclusion of my room at the National. I would have to get used to it, however, as life was now going to be very different.

Looking back, I realise that this toughening-up process was vital to my rehabilitation, but at the time, it seemed cruel and I admit I was sorry for myself. There were far fewer nurses in attendance and I became very aware of my helplessness and complete dependence on other people.

Ambulant patients were kind and often came over and helped me, giving me drinks of water, letters to read and turning the pages of my book. Reading in the lung was a frustratingly slow process, as the book was placed on a perspex screen over my head and I had no way of turning my own pages.

I found the ward noisy and distracting and concentrated thought was out of the question. Routine dictated that my day should start at 5.15 a.m. with a tepid wash and attention of pressure areas. The rest of the ward was then awakened, which put paid to any further sleep, and I just had to lie and wait until breakfast at 7.15. It was a good thing for the nurse that I ate little of this. She really did not have the time to give it to me and I was always glad when there was an 'up' patient who could relieve her of this tedious chore. My first day ended at 11 p.m. and, by that time, I had had several other shocks. I learnt that my teeth would be cleaned for the last time of the day at 3.30 in the afternoon, and that I would have only two bed baths a week.

I had led a coddled, sheltered existence at the National, and had never before been away from the ward without my breathing apparatus and a nurse beside me. Here, I was expected to go to Treatment Block for physiotherapy and the X-ray department in the hands of just a porter. At first I was terrified, but they were marvellous men. They understood, and allayed my feelings of panic by laughing and joking.

For the first time since my illness, I met disabled people in large numbers. I was more extensively paralysed than many of them, but we all had one aim in life—to get back into the world and live as normally as possible. For me, the way back seemed quite impossible and I was often depressed at the prospect before me. Twice a day, I was taken to Treatment Block where the atmosphere was wonderful. Everyone worked with cheerful optimism, patiently retraining limbs extensively damaged through accident, illness or congenital deformity. The majority of patients being rehabilitated were those disabled, like myself, as a result of poliomyelitis and there was a great spirit of camaraderie amongst us. I discovered that others were also finding it hard to accept disablement. Somehow, this was a comfort to me. I wasn't the only one fighting this lone battle.

The physiotherapists were most understanding about my problems and depressions, but it took many years to fully accept the fact that I had been irrevocably immobilised. The odds seemed too great. I had black days when I despaired of ever doing anything with my life. On these days, I remained in the ward, unable to face the ever cheerful physiotherapists and the jolly atmosphere that always prevailed in their department. I longed for solitude so that I could get over my depression. I did not want sympathy. I just wanted to be left alone.

The nurses, though very young, were sweet and wanted desperately to help. They *did* help me, just by being so kind. I was suffering from self-pity, which was helping no-one, least of all myself. Only I could conquer these recurring bouts of depression. If only I could *do* something.

Twice a week, I had a session with the occupational therapist who made me stencil tiles. My arm was suspended, as for typing, from a beam over my bed and a paint brush was strapped to my fingers. The therapist then guided my arm into the paint pot and I swung it to and fro, hoping desperately to hit the tile. I usually missed! The tiles then went to be fired and the following week I would be shown the result. I thought they were horrible. All the colours had changed and looked drab and not a bit artistic. Everyone, however, was very kind and encouraging, but I thought the whole thing a useless waste of time. Being so dependent on the therapist, I felt no sense of achievement. As soon as I left Stanmore, I discarded this method of painting. If only I had tried to use my mouth then for reading and painting, I would have saved myself years of frustration. I always thought a stick in my mouth would impede my breathing, and I also disliked the idea of looking odd. I *was* disabled, but did not want to *appear* disabled.

It was now quite definite that I would remain helpless for the rest of my life. The point of staying at Stanmore was to strengthen me physically and to improve my equipment. First of all, I had to graduate from the big iron lung to a more portable cuirass-type of respirator. Two doctors were working on it and this was now nearing completion. The cuirass, made of light-weight plastic and surrounded by a soft, spongy rubber seal, straps closely round my chest. It is connected by a hose to a small motor which works the bellows, and acts in the same way as an iron lung, thus still giving me mechanical artificial respiration. When it arrived eventually, it took me a week or so to learn to sleep in this new machine, but it was lovely to be in a bed again. At last I was out of my tomb.

Through the day, I breathe consciously, using the accessory muscles in my neck, giving me the appearance of being constantly out of breath. As I am no longer able to breathe automatically, I will never again sleep without a machine.

I had to acquire a rocking bed so that I could rest some part of the day. Also a suitable wheelchair. The kind of chair I needed was unobtainable in this country, but one was eventually brought over from America through various helpful friends.[1] This is a wonderful chair. It enables me to be lowered to the horizontal position as well as being propped upright.

To get me used to living out of hospital, I spent weekends with Janet and David.[2] The first time I left the ward, the

---

[1] This chair is now manufactured in this country.

[2] Janet had had a non-paralytic form of polio. John had considerable residual paralysis and, when he was fourteen, had to undergo a spinal fusion operation at Stanmore.

ambulance was late coming for me. I got so worked up and excited that I shot a temperature which, fortunately, was ignored. It was wonderful to be in a house again and Janet and David were marvellous, making light of all the extra work I must have made. I had a bed in their living-room and they had a bell fixed to ring in their bedroom. In fact, they did everything to make me comfortable. I always enjoyed being there and loathed Sunday nights and the awful return to hospital.

There were many frustrating delays over the accumulation of my equipment, but by the autumn of 1955, more than two years after my first admission into hospital, I was discharged and taken home to my parents. The glorious air of Kent made a noticeable difference to my breathing, and the Old School House was peaceful and homely after the austerity to which I had become accustomed. Here too, I had the use of a ground floor room, this time the dining-room, but I still needed considerable nursing as I was only in my chair for about three hours a day. The district nurse called every morning and a physiotherapist twice a week, but otherwise we had little attendant help.

I very soon realised what a tax I was on my parents and sister, Alison. With the onset of winter, storms sometimes brought down the overhead cables, cutting off the electricity supply. Then, someone had to get up and take me out of my respirator. This round-the-clock responsibility was obviously too much for them and after Christmas, I was readmitted to the National.

Matron had told me always to think of this hospital as my second home, and I have since been back many times. This return was memorable for my first outing to a theatre. Two doctors decided to take me to the ballet at the Royal Opera House, Covent Garden. They discussed and planned it all most carefully with the Theatre Management, and I attended an evening performance in which Dame Margot Fonteyn was dancing the 'Firebird'.

I spent the day quietly in my respirator, but my excitement was very hard to suppress. This return to former haunts was charged with emotion and has left a very vivid memory. Everyone at the hospital was anxious that I should enjoy it. My only worry was that, in my excitement, I would forget to breathe!

The St. John's ambulance came early. I had to be in place before the rest of the audience was admitted. This has since been the arrangement at every theatre and it is always a thrill to be the first person in the auditorium.

As we drew up at the entrance, Arnott, one of my ex-dancing partners, now a member of the Royal Ballet, stepped forward and greeted me. I was delighted, and he made my first reappearance in public much easier. He seemed so thrilled at having me there, and chatted enthusiastically as I was carried sedately up the grand staircase, through the crush bar and into my box in the grand tier. His presence eased my nerves and quashed my feelings of nostalgia. For the first time, I met the Commissionaires, Sergeant Martin and Mr. Posstlethwaite, those imposing figures in top hats and red coats that grace the doors of the Opera House. The box was minute, but I had an excellent view of the stage. The theatre was as I had always remembered it, beautiful and full of romance. All went well. I did not forget to breathe, nor did I get upset at seeing the ballet again. I had a most enjoyable and happy evening.

Dame Margot was unable to visit me, but on the following day, I received a letter from her saying that she hoped I had enjoyed the performance. I had something else the next day too—a streaming cold. I was confined to bed and stuffed with antibiotics.

I am grateful to those far-seeing doctors for arranging this wonderful evening, and to everyone who made it all so easy for me.

. . . . .

I have now lost count of the number of theatre trips I have made. All of them have been enjoyable and many memorable. Everywhere, I have met with tremendous courtesy and kindness and am often thoroughly spoilt by the management. I receive 'Royal' attention, but I have one privilege more than the Queen—I do not even walk up the stairs!

The Public Relations Officer at Covent Garden has often arranged for me to see special dress-rehearsals and to renew old friendships, to meet members of the ballet in my box and have photographs taken with them in the crush bar as souvenirs. At the Royal Albert Hall, the Manager arranged for me to meet Sir Malcolm Sargent several times after the Christmas Carol concerts. I must have reminded him of a very sad occasion in his life as he lost a daughter with poliomyelitis, but he was always friendly and very easy to talk to.

I find a great welcome awaiting me at art galleries too. Kindly commissionaires come over and say,

'Hello! You back again?'

'How are you? You look a lot better than you did last time you came.'

If the gallery is crowded, as it was at the Picasso exhibition at the Tate, there is no queueing for me. There's a cry of 'Mind your backs!' and I'm in.

When I wrote to Sir Antony Blunt, Purveyor of the Queen's pictures, to ask if it was possible for me to visit the Queen's gallery, he told me to be at Buckingham Palace at a certain time, one morning. I was surprised to see him draw up opposite me in a taxi. He personally escorted me round the Gallery, talking to me about the various prints and pictures. He was utterly charming and most interesting.

It is amazing how many people contribute to the enjoyment of my outings, often quite unintentionally. Once, when I visited the Summer exhibition at the Royal Academy, my escort was the local Curate—tall, young and bearded. He wore his cassock, and every time I wanted to study the catalogue he knelt down beside me. On rising, there was great dusting and brushing of knees. We must have made an odd couple and were obviously very distracting.

Another time, there was a tiny child who said, 'Mummy, look at that lady in her pram!' pointing at me. The mother was very embarrassed, but I loved the remark.

Police and traffic wardens who turn a blind eye and make concessions for me: cheerful strangers often ready to help; my drivers and attendants always willing to enter into the fun of it. To all of them, my gratitude is unbounded.

With my parents and Eamonn Andrews on 'This is Your Life'   BBC

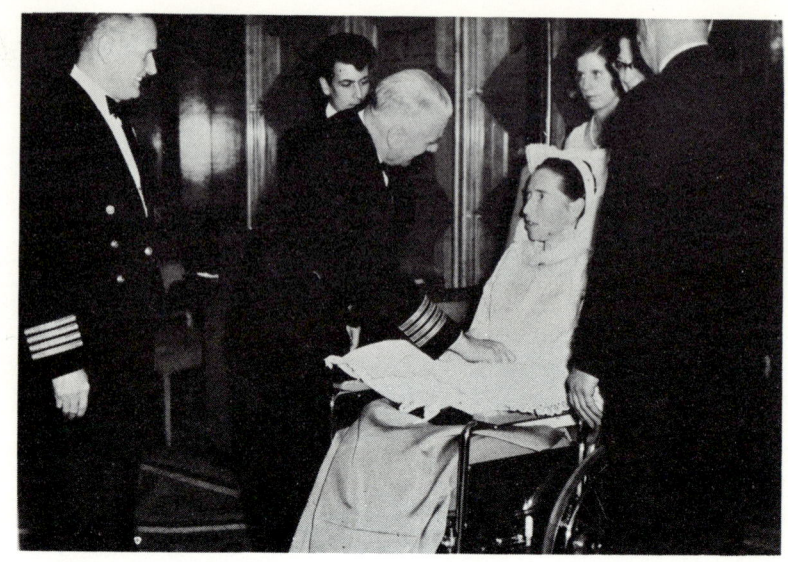

At the Captain's Party on board the Mauretania

Beside the River Jordan

6

SECOND CAREER: MOUTH PAINTING

My life was filled with long periods of idleness and I still suffered bouts of appalling depression. I was angry and frustrated at this overwhelming sense of uselessness and must have been a very difficult person. Kind friends tried to invent gadgets to make me more independent, but I had so little movement that these usually ended up by being tremendously elaborate pieces of equipment which the staff had no time to fix. These lay idle, cluttering up the ward, and I was a most unpopular patient as a result.

I was shunted from hospital to hospital, on to the family, then back again into hospital. This constant moving continued for several years, until I was transferred to the British Polio Fellowship Hostel in 1957. Here something happened that changed my life, that enabled me to make the much needed mental adjustment to my disability, and which gave me new hope and a real purpose in life.

At this Hostel, there was no staff on duty in the afternoon, and unless I went back to bed and had my arm suspended from my overhead beam, I could do nothing. Two other residents with very extensive paralysis used mouth sticks to turn the pages of their books, and I decided to see if I could use one. I found it awkward at first, but gradually improvised, and improved one to suit my capabilities. I had a lightweight stick with a rubber thimble on the end and found, to my amazement, that it did not impede my breathing. I have read this way ever since. Newspapers and very shiny magazines are impossible to cope with, but what do they matter if I have books? These come in plenty from the hospital or housebound section of the Public Library.

The Hostel had an association of 'Friends', contributing in various ways to the well-being and comfort of the residents. They arranged outings, lent their cars so that we could go shopping, to the theatre or to church. In fact, they made life pleasant and exciting for us. One of these friends sent in some boxes of oil paints, hoping that some of us might find them useful. On two afternoons a week, some ladies came in to help us.

I can recall most vividly my first tentative steps in painting. Rosie was helping me and it took us quite a long time to work out how to get the canvas on a level with my face. I could make no movement towards it—the canvas had to be brought to me. She dragged a nearby table in front of me and piled up some books. These were all different shapes and sizes, so it was anything but a stable structure. On top of this, she placed my little wooden reading stand and then put the canvas board in place.

'There!' she said. 'Now, what are you going to paint?'

The canvas looked very white and empty and I had not a clue how to start, nor had I a notion of what to paint. I glanced across the room at two other residents. Vicky, who painted with her hands, was putting the finishing touches to a still-life, and John, though helpless, was painting by mouth and vigorously completing a seascape. I looked back at my canvas. It was blank—blank as my mind. In desperation, I said I would paint a landscape. Rosie squeezed some cobalt blue and white on to the palette and started mixing, adding turps and a little oil. She soon had what I thought a pleasant colour.

'We want a touch of red', she said.

I glanced out of the window.

'Red!' I thought. 'She's crazy! There's no red in a blue sky!'

SECOND CAREER: MOUTH PAINTING

But when I looked back at the palette, sure enough, that touch of alizarin had made all the difference. I realised there was an awful lot to learn.

Rose took the longest brush she could find, loaded it with paint and put it in my mouth. I could not reach the canvas, so very gingerly, the column of books was pushed towards me (and towards the edge of the table!) It wobbled, then crashed to the floor, knocking my brush into my lap. There was paint everywhere!

I was weary by this time and had to lie down and rest for a few minutes. Tea arrived, so it was at least another half an hour before I was set up and we tried again.

There was my canvas, staring reproachfully at me, white and empty, but this time, Rose held it steady and I started to tackle the sky. The brush was only nine inches long so I felt rather cross-eyed as the thick, blue paint ate up that accusing white surface. The exertion made me very breathless and red in the face. I dribbled and chewed on the brush, and eventually snapped a bit off the end, which meant we had to start again, moving everything nearer.

My sky looked horrible, not a bit realistic. It looked like the work of an artistic chimpanzee, but in spite of the hazards and pitfalls and difficulties, I had enjoyed the afternoon. There was little to show for all the time and effort expended, but it had been fun and I looked forward to our next painting session.

Looking back to these early days of my art career when we had to improvise equipment, I found it incredibly difficult to get the paint on the canvas. Most of it went on the floor, on myself and on my helpers, who left, smelling strongly of turpentine. They were very patient, however, and if they felt their task was hopeless, they never showed me their feelings.

Week after week, we persevered, and gradually, my daubing took shape. I produced a picture—my first picture—'Three tomatoes on a Wedgwood-blue plate'. This was painted entirely from imagination and must have started off accidentally, as I am certain I had no preconceived idea about the subject matter. My helper this time was Kit. She mixed the colours, and I expect made a nice tomato red one day. That triggered off the whole thing. I know the Wedgewood blue plate was my idea and I remember getting very excited as she gradually got the exact colour I had in mind. I had no idea then how to obtain different colours, and it was wonderful for me to find someone who could interpret my ideas so exactly. It was a unique partnership at a very opportune moment, as our artistic feeling and taste seemed to merge. I am proud to think that she now has the painting hanging in her Kensington home and has the decor of the room to match.

A few months later, I was transferred back to the National Hospital where Dorothy Cockayne, the occupational therapist, started to equip me for what is now my career. She is an aesthetic, delicate-looking person and has suffered several severe illnesses, including a long period of blindness. Having this personal experience of helplessness, she knows what it is like to be dependent on other people and has great sympathy and understanding of the problems involved. One of her best pieces of advice to me was, 'When people don't understand what you are asking them to do, try asking it in a different way. It doesn't always work, but it is worth trying.'

She designed an easel that fitted on to a table placed on the arms of my wheelchair. This was adjustable and had four glass pots in front containing paint—blue, yellow, red and white. But as I had no way of cleaning my own brush, these jars soon contained the same muddy grey mixture! There was also a small palette with a clip-on pot of oil and a holder for my brushes. This easel was a great improvement on the pile of books with the canvas propped precariously on top, and I used it for many months.

After Christmas, I went to one of the Cheshire Foundation Homes where I struggled along on my own for three weeks, painting mostly fishes in reeds and imaginative landscapes. The results were anything but satisfactory, but I was gaining control over my brush and could put more paint on the canvas and less on the floor.

On a snowy day in February I was moved again, this time to the National Hospital Convalescent Home in Finchley. Here, Miss Cockayne managed to visit me twice a week and we made some further improvements to my equipment. One of the biggest problems has always been the lengthening of the paint brushes. For me, a comfortable distance from my eyes to the canvas is sixteen inches, so this means adding several inches on to the handle of the brushes. These must weigh as little as possible and be treated to withstand the tremendous pressure put on them by tightly clamped jaws. One idea Miss Cockayne had was to adapt some old-fashioned ivory glove stretchers, and with immense patience, rubbed these down and shaped them into brush ends. They did service for many years but were far too heavy. Now I use wooden dowelling, quarter-inch diameter, tipped with dental plastic, or strong but light perspex rods covered with Magill's tubing, which gives me a good grip and therefore, greater control.

All this time though, I felt I was only groping my way through the intricacies and mysteries of painting. No-one seemed to be taking my desire to learn art seriously. Why did nobody teach me? Time was passing and I knew little more now than I did when I started eight months before. I was not interested in just keeping myself occupied. I needed to get my teeth into something useful. Here was something I felt I could do and I wanted to do it well.

When I went back home to Kent, I talked over my problem with Dr. Boulden. Being an artist himself, he understood and, through the East Kent Art Society, found me a teacher, Rosemary Howard. This is when I felt I really started to learn something about art. I was thirsting for knowledge and absorbed her lessons greedily. After four years of idleness, this was so exciting and I worked hard. My improvement, however, was exasperatingly slow, but I began to know what I wanted to do.

I was very restricted in many ways but realised that, if I worked hard enough, it was possible for me to produce pictures comparable to an artist with no disabilities. It would take me longer to do this. It would make me angry, depressed, disheartened, but with effort, I could really achieve something in life. What I did *not* foresee was that painting would enable me to earn enough money to run a flat, a car, and to live a fairly normal life again. These rewards came several years later. At the start of my career, I knew only that painting eased my pent-up feelings, helped me overcome that terrible craving to move, releasing me spiritually so that I forgot my paralysed body and found I was moving, dancing, creating again.

Rosemary came twice a week, riding her bicycle from Walmer. It was a pleasure to see her; always beautifully dressed, always bringing 'something exciting' in her basket, either to paint, something new to try, or something to show me. One of her hobbies is puppet-making and, for several weeks, she was accompanied by a different 'character' exquisitely made and most entertaining. It must have been quite an ordeal for a person as sensitive as Rosemary to make these regular visits, but she achieved far more than she set out to do. She taught me the rudiments of painting and all the things I was longing to learn, but she also boosted my morale, often raised my flagging spirits and renewed my enthusiasm.

SECOND CAREER: MOUTH PAINTING 57

Sometimes I felt so disheartened that, without her sympathetic and gentle encouragement, I would no doubt have given up.

Each day, my parents or Alison set out my paints for me and I sloshed and daubed and persevered, gradually gaining more control. I became ambitious and made an attempt to paint figures.

'You want to run before you can walk!' was Rosemary's comment, but she gave me a lesson on figure drawing, and the following week, one of her pupils was posing for me.

It *was* dancing figures I was seeking. I think I was only dimly aware of this but, there they were, gradually emerging from my brush.

'Very un-anatomical', commented my father!

And of course, he was right. But this was a branch of painting that I, as a dancer, could correct. Only the ballet world would know if my figures were dancing. Painters could tell me about my composition and how to achieve this and that effect, but I was back in my role of teacher, and only I could perfect the performers on my canvas. I was surprised that, after years of immobility, I could still 'feel' the movements I was trying to portray. I had not forgotten how to dance. I found myself dancing again in a new medium.

Joy in my work is always fleeting. Inevitably, I soon detect faults and feel dissatisfied with my efforts. The more one learns of any of the arts, the more critical one becomes, and I have often ruined paintings by trying to improve them. Invariably, my most successful paintings have been dashed off in a carefree few moments.

Winter was again approaching, with its inevitable storms and gales felling the overhead electric cables and causing sleepless nights to my family. It was time I went back into hospital.

7

THE WAY OUT

When I first left hospital, I found this was the beginning of many new problems. I was left with only slight movement in my right hand and part of my neck. I have to be fed, washed, clothed; sat in my chair, put to bed and into my respirator. I am now very thin, so my bony pressure areas need regular nursing attention, and my body needs frequent adjustments for comfort and variation of position. Being helpless means that it is impossible for me to be left for any length of time. It might be only a fly on my nose, or a wasp on my hand, but I do need somebody within calling distance. When I am living at home, this constant availability puts a tremendous strain on limited staff and the problems seem insurmountable.

Dr. Boulden approached the local Medical Officer of Health, Dr. Lynch, and discussed with him the possibility of my being admitted to a hospital nearer home. Dr. Lynch, a quiet, gentle Irishman, quickly sized up the situation. He was sympathetic and very understanding, and most anxious to help. He offered me a bed at the Dover Isolation Hospital, where he said I would receive enough attention and help to enable me to continue my art studies. I had started on my second career and an inner driving force compelled me to go on. My creative desires had to be satisfied and, if I did not paint each day, I felt miserably frustrated.

I was ambitious to make something of my life and to use the talent that had been given me. I was not content to be idle all day, though I realised that the harder I worked, the more work I made for those looking after me.

I hated changes and dreaded going to the Isolation Hospital. It was only a small place situated on a hillside overlooking the town, with distant views of Dover harbour and the castle. I moved in at the end of October, arriving complete with bed, bedding, respirator, art equipment and typewriter. I broke all the rules for a normal isolation case. There were six cubicles each side of a central kitchen opening on to wide verandahs. Each room was about twelve feet square with glass sides. I had two of them, one for my bed and night equipment, the other I used as a studio. The nurses were wonderfully kind and co-operative and soon had everything sorted out. There was little change of staff, and it was not long before they were all conversant with my daily routine, which was to make life much easier for me.

I was put in my chair just after nine o'clock each morning. My equipment was set out for me and I worked for a couple of hours. The nurses coped with the cleaning of the brushes and palette when I had finished. Rosemary came over two afternoons a week to give me lessons, and these regular painting sessions enabled me to make some considerable progress.

At Christmas, I designed a card. I sketched a single figure in arabesque in sepia colour on a white background. Comparing it with my present work, it was very unanatomical and not particularly seasonable, but I had a hundred printed locally for my friends. The one I sent to Kit, who had helped me with my first painting, was noticed by a London reporter, Roy Nash, who was interviewing her about some charity work. As he was interested, she showed him the 'Three Tomatoes on a Wedgwood-blue plate', and he decided to come to Dover to meet me. The hospital authorities gave him permission for an interview and he came down one afternoon. Rosemary came over early and set out my paintings as attractively as possible. The nurses took extra trouble with my appearance, but I must confess that I was very nervous as I awaited his arrival.

Soon after two o'clock, a sturdy, dark-haired figure, wearing hornrimmed spectacles, walked up the drive.

'I think that's him', said Rosemary, and went out to meet him. He had an open jolly face with dimples and a small cleft in his chin. He was charming and sympathetic and I found it easy to talk to him. Our meeting turned out to be most enjoyable and not at all the ordeal I had thought it would be. He had arranged for me to be photographed with some of my paintings and, a few days later, the following feature appeared:

THE WONDERFUL STORY OF A GIRL'S COURAGE

The world this evening is a private world, one in which I hesitate to intrude. Once it was public, this world of Elizabeth Twistington Higgins. Applause, limelight, bouquets, the wave of admiration that sweeps across the footlights to greet a well-poised arabesque—as a ballet dancer, Elizabeth knew them all.

At 14, she saw a theatre curtain go up on the moonlit mystery of Les Sylphides and knew she wanted to be a dancer. Countless schoolgirls, slipping upstairs after homework to pirouette before the bathroom mirror and look once more through their hoard of 239 pictures of Dame Margot, dream this dream.

For Surgeon's daughter, Elizabeth, it came true. In her twenties, after graduation from Sadlers' Wells School, she danced—as Elizabeth Scott—through Song of Norway and King's Rhapsody in London's West End.

Then, six years ago, polio robbed her of the use of her limbs. Her battle with the illness was long; she spent two years in an iron lung.

Today, although she has made remarkable progress, the world of Elizabeth Twistington Higgins is still a world of hospital rooms and a wheelchair. But it is also a world of paint and canvas, of colour and line. For Elizabeth—in her early thirties now—has learnt to paint with her mouth.

I heard about her pictures by chance and wrote asking if I might call to talk about her work and herself. A refusal would not have surprised me. Consider the contrast between the life of a dancer in which movement is everything and the life of a polio victim in which practically all movement is impossible. It is a cruel contrast, too cruel, some might think, for anyone who has experienced it, to speak of it.

But Elizabeth sent a swift reply, inviting me to see her at Dover Isolation Hospital. She wrote the letter herself—on an electric typewriter, which she operates by jabbing the keys with a stick controlled by the slight movement of her right hand, all the limb-movement polio has left her.

Two things impressed me tremendously about this young woman who smiled and joked in her wheelchair. One was her determination to overcome physical handicap; the other was the quality of her pictures, which were good.

The Star,
16 April 1959

For someone as isolated as I was, this publicity was a great help. Roy Nash's enthusiasm was very encouraging and we have met many times since that first interview. He is always one jump ahead of me, always suggesting that I attempt what I consider to be impossible.

In the spring of 1959, Rosemary arranged my first one-man show at the Dover Public Library. She hung about a dozen paintings on black velvet in a glass-fronted case in the entrance hall. She painted lovely big posters and mounted Roy Nash's article in a prominent position. For the first time, I sold my work to the general public.

I was pushed down to the Library in my wheelchair (no mean feat as the hills in Dover are very steep). I was surprised and delighted to be received by the Head Librarian and presented with a bouquet. The exhibition, though very small, roused considerable local interest, and it was good to know that my work gave pleasure to people. The struggles and the heartaches had not been in vain.

Some time during the summer, Jenny Poynting, my night

special from the National, brought her husband, John Ripley, to visit me. John's printing firm specialised in fine art reproduction which was singularly fortunate for me. He selected three of my designs and offered to print them as Christmas cards. The results were quite pleasing and I decided to try and sell them. With the help of a young student from the Technical College, we sent out nearly 3,000 cards. This, though very encouraging, involved a tremendous amount of labour and I decided never to do it again.

Roy Nash was anxious that my work should be seen outside Kent. He took some of my paintings to the exhibitions officer at London's Royal Festival Hall. This visit resulted in a request for thirty-five more pictures to show during the Festival Ballet's Christmas season of *The Nutcracker*. It seemed a terrifyingly large order and I was very diffident about accepting. Today, I should probably give an outright refusal but, in 1960, I was persuaded to try and had the temerity to show about fifty paintings in all. They were hung, unframed, on coloured panels in the Queen's reception room. I managed to go up to London and see them for myself. I felt quite overawed viewing my work in such majestic surroundings.

Several exciting things happened as a result of this exhibition. One of my sketches—two dancers on a black background—was used as the outside cover of a medical magazine. The Managing Director of the Medici Society bought the reproduction rights of this painting and printed it as a birthday card. Since then, the Medici Society have acquired several of my designs for use as prints and greetings cards.

Two of my other ballet designs went to the Cunard Line to be used as menu cards on their transatlantic liners, and Toc 'H' asked me to design a special Christmas card for them that year. One was sent to their Patron, Queen Elizabeth the Queen Mother, who sent a letter of appreciation.

After all this excitement, I felt rather flat on my return

THE WAY OUT

to the Isolation Hospital, but I was not allowed to slack. The head of the Dover Art School, who had helped me with advice and lessons on several occasions, suggested that I should hold a one-man show at the School. He mounted and exhibited my work. The Press were most encouraging and I sold a considerable number of pictures.

Each summer, I sent work to the East Kent Art Society's exhibition in Canterbury, where my work is judged alongside artists who are not disabled. The first year, I submitted a small painting of 'Apple Blossom'. When I visited the exhibition, we had the utmost difficulty in finding this picture. It was hung, very inauspiciously, round a corner all on its own. But there, on the bottom, was a red dot! It had been sold. And the person who bought it had no idea that it had been painted by a mouth painter. I felt thrilled. I wanted my work to be judged for its merit, with no consideration at all for my handicap.

I also sent paintings to an annual exhibition for disabled artists in America. Thanks to this show and my menu cards on the Cunard Liner, my work was becoming known on both sides of the Alantic.

Roy Nash felt that it should reach an even wider public. He wrote to the B.B.C. programme, Monitor. They replied that his letter 'had been passed to the appropriate department'. Roy had no idea when he sent that letter that it was going to lead me into one of the most exciting and nerve-racking half-hours of my life.

8

TELEVISION

My birthday in 1961 is firmly etched in my memory. I was asked by the B.B.C. to appear in 'Town and Around', a daily magazine programme about the South East of England. When they suggested that I went to London for the interview, I was a bit suspicious. In normal circumstances, a mobile camera team would have come to Dover. My suspicions were well-founded; this was only a ruse to get me to appear on the weekly programme 'This is Your Life', which gave a glimpse into the lives of celebrated or interesting people. I was amazed that they should consider me a suitable subject.

An appearance on 'This is Your Life' was supposed to come as a complete surprise, but my doctor had advised the producer not to spring a sudden shock on me. I *was* shocked. I burst into tears. I felt I could not face my friends and relations saying kind and flattering things about me for half an hour. Overwhelming kindness always upsets me.

I told Matron I could not do it. She seemed very disappointed but I think she understood. I was glad she was the only person who witnessed my emotional outburst. She left, saying that the decision was entirely up to me; I was to think it over and let her know in the morning.

This bombshell interrupted a painting lesson with Rosemary and had completely shattered my powers of concentration. There was no more work that afternoon.

I discovered that Rosemary was already in on the secret, and she spent the rest of the afternoon calming me down. She told me that, of the four lives prepared for the following week, three had left the country. If I did not appear, the programme would either have to be cancelled or a repeat performance shown. She was very persuasive. I felt I could not let everyone down and accepted the challenge, though reluctantly. I had accepted challenges before, but this one scared me stiff. In the theatre, I would have given my bottom dollar for this kind of publicity. Now, I was in a wheelchair. I did not want to appear before an audience.

The nurses knew that something was troubling me but, as I was under a vow of silence, it was impossible for me to communicate with them. I could not eat or sleep or concentrate; my thoughts were focused entirely on the ordeal ahead. My mind was so preoccupied that I never even thought of buying anything special to wear on this great occasion. Looking back, I am still amazed at myself—it was so unlike me. I felt sick with anxiety and nerves and the next four days seemed endless.

On the fifth of November, I was formally admitted to the Observation Ward of the Middlesex Hospital in London. Here too, secrecy prevailed and I was obviously a rather mysterious patient. I was under the care of the R.M.O., and his young Houseman thought I was an interesting case. After asking me a lot of questions about my illness, he looked incredulously at me and said, 'You're a living miracle!'

This was his first meeting with someone who had had respiratory polio.

Early the next morning, the B.B.C. took possession of my room. Everything was moved out of the way; cameras brought in, cables laid, lights fixed, sound tested; the interviewer, Nancy Wise, came in and we were on the air.

The conversation that followed was spontaneous and went off quite well, apart from one rather awkward moment.

'Do you miss the world of ballet?'

For a second, I was completely taken aback by such an obvious query, and sharply retorted,

'Of *course* I do!'

This was not very polite of me and Nancy must have felt terrible having asked such a tactless question. I have always been a volatile and emotional person. If only I could react more slowly and had greater control over my emotions, I would so often save others from being hurt and embarrassed.

At the end of the interview, Nancy said to me, 'As it is your birthday Elizabeth, the B.B.C. has prepared a surprise for you.'

She turned to face the door and in walked Eamonn Andrews.

After a few words of greeting, he asked me if I would come to the Television Theatre that evening and see what other surprises the B.B.C. had in store for me.

I spent the afternoon resting in my respirator. I was being washed and dressed for the evening performance when our pre-recorded interview was shown in 'Town and Around'. I did not see myself, nor did I hear Eamonn Andrews say that, for the first time, they were breaking the usual rule of silence for the evening's performance of 'This is Your Life'. Owing to my disabilities, it had been decided to warn me beforehand that I would be appearing.

The R.M.O. came to see that I was feeling all right before I set off in the ambulance for the theatre. We got there with only five minutes to spare. Fortunately, I did not know we were cutting it as fine as this, or I would have been in a terrible state.

I was backed down a ramp directly on to stage level. There, one of my dancing partners from *Song of Norway* greeted me and gave me a birthday present—the first and only one that day. I only appreciated the thoughtfulness of this gesture when everything was over.

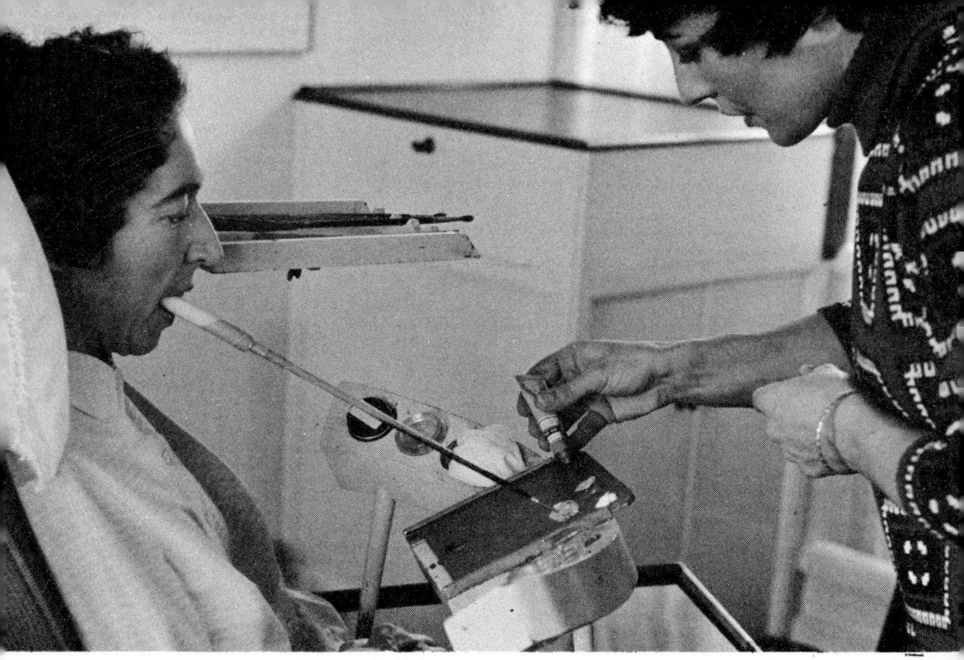

1. Setting out the paints

2. Selecting a brush

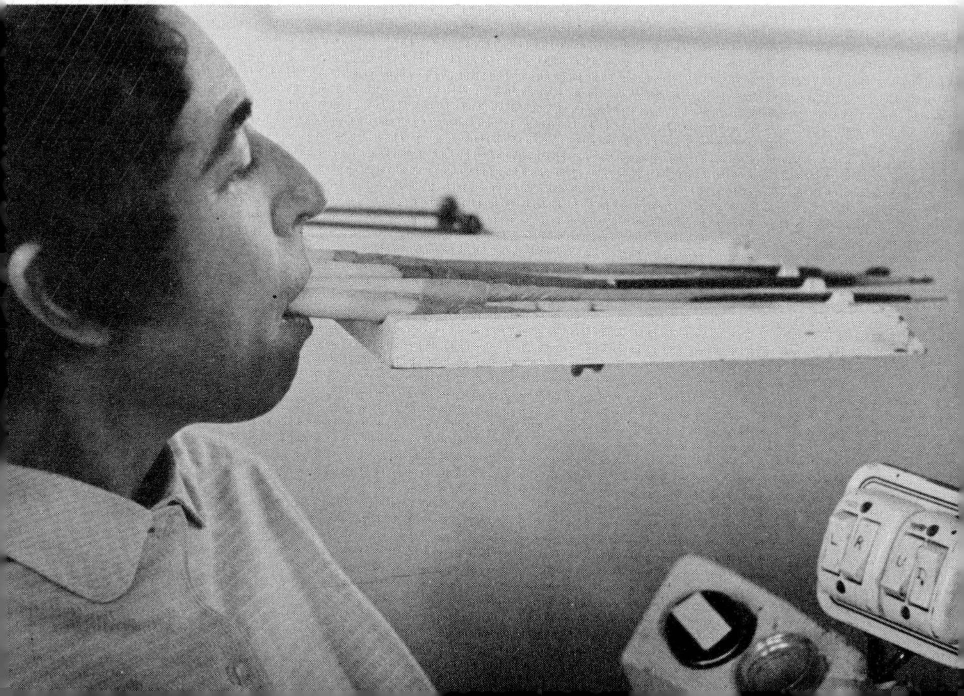

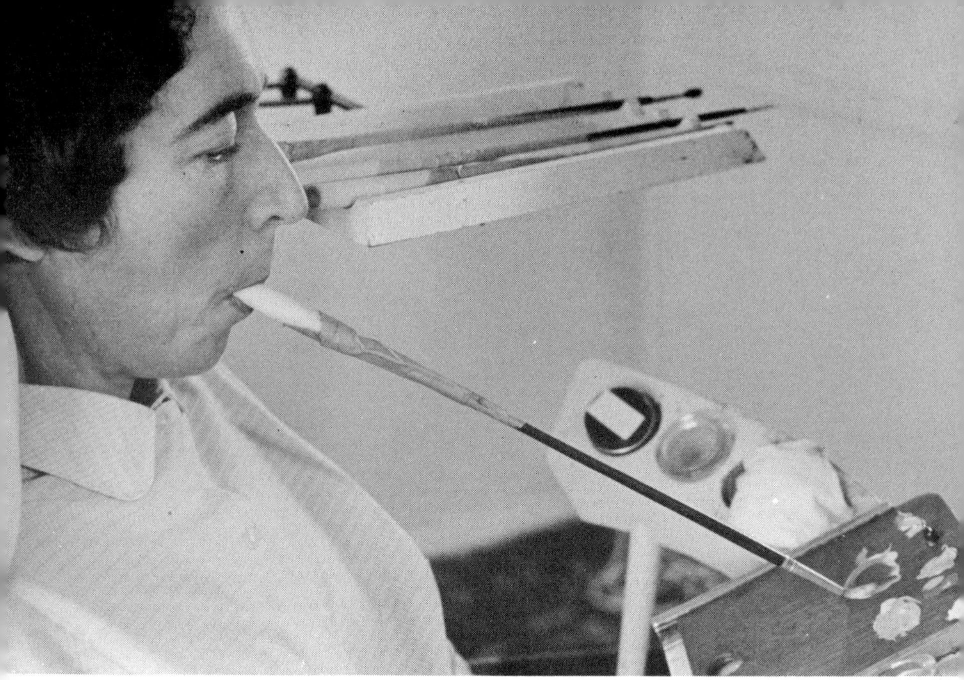

3. *Mixing the colours*

4. *Washing the brushes*

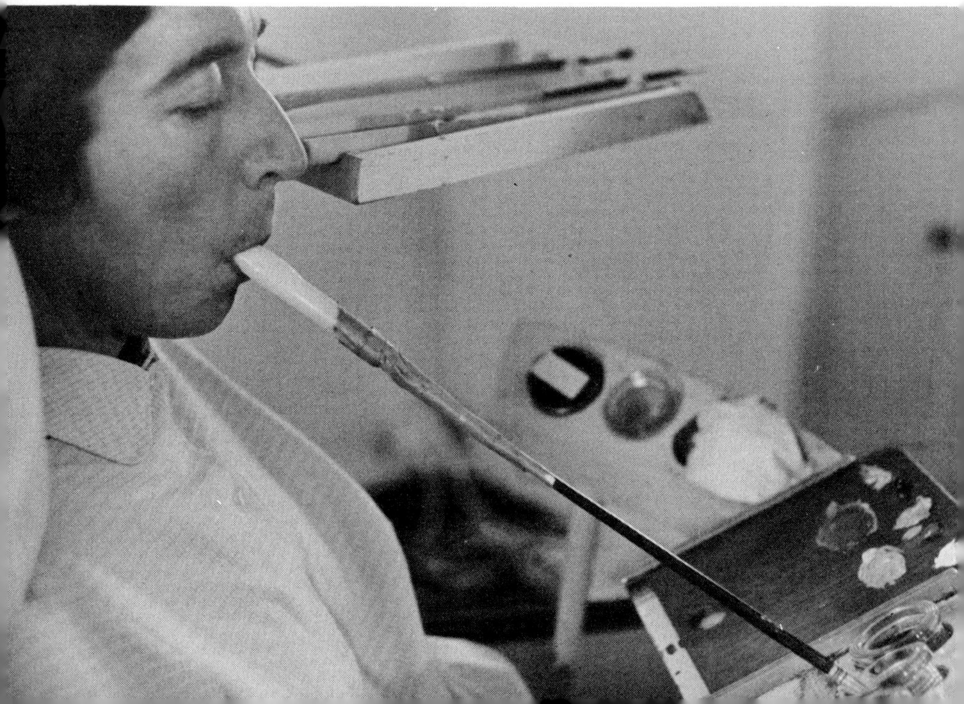

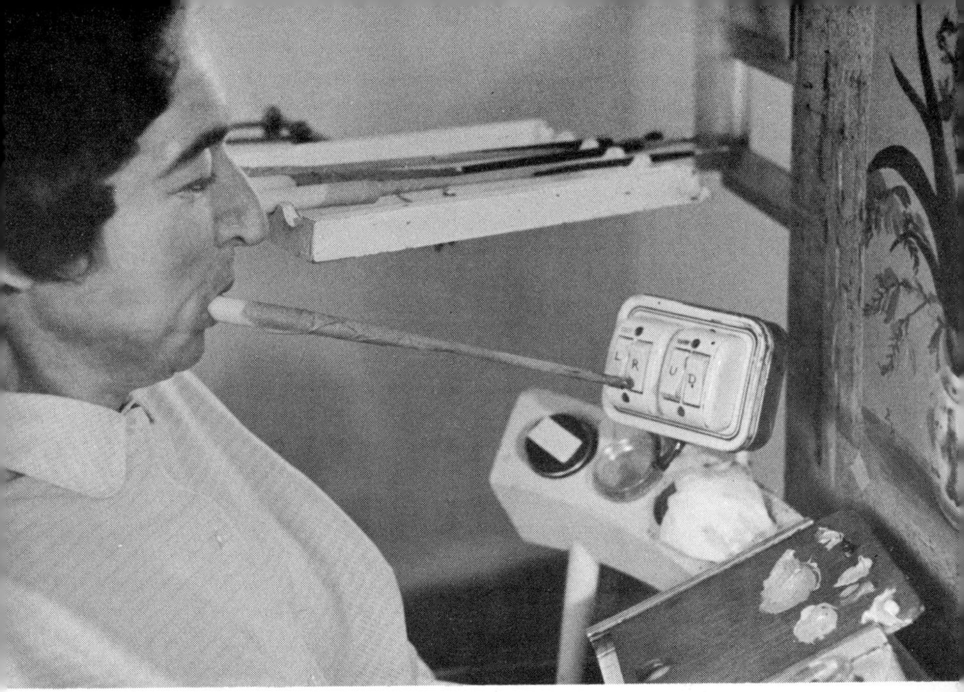

5. *Pushing the button to move the easel*

6. *Painting*   *Sequence of six photos :* MERLYN SEVERN

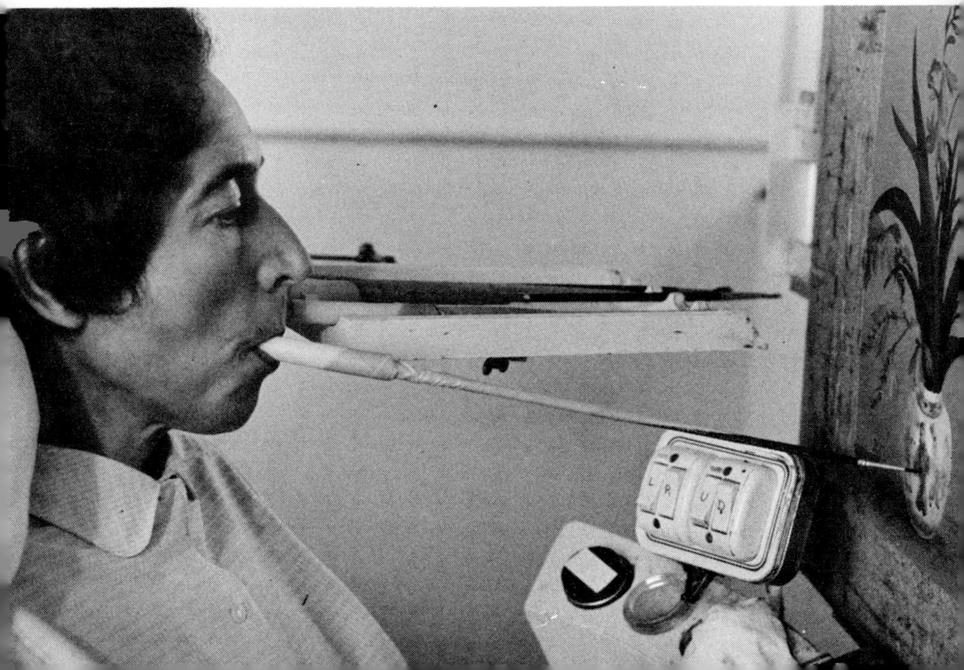

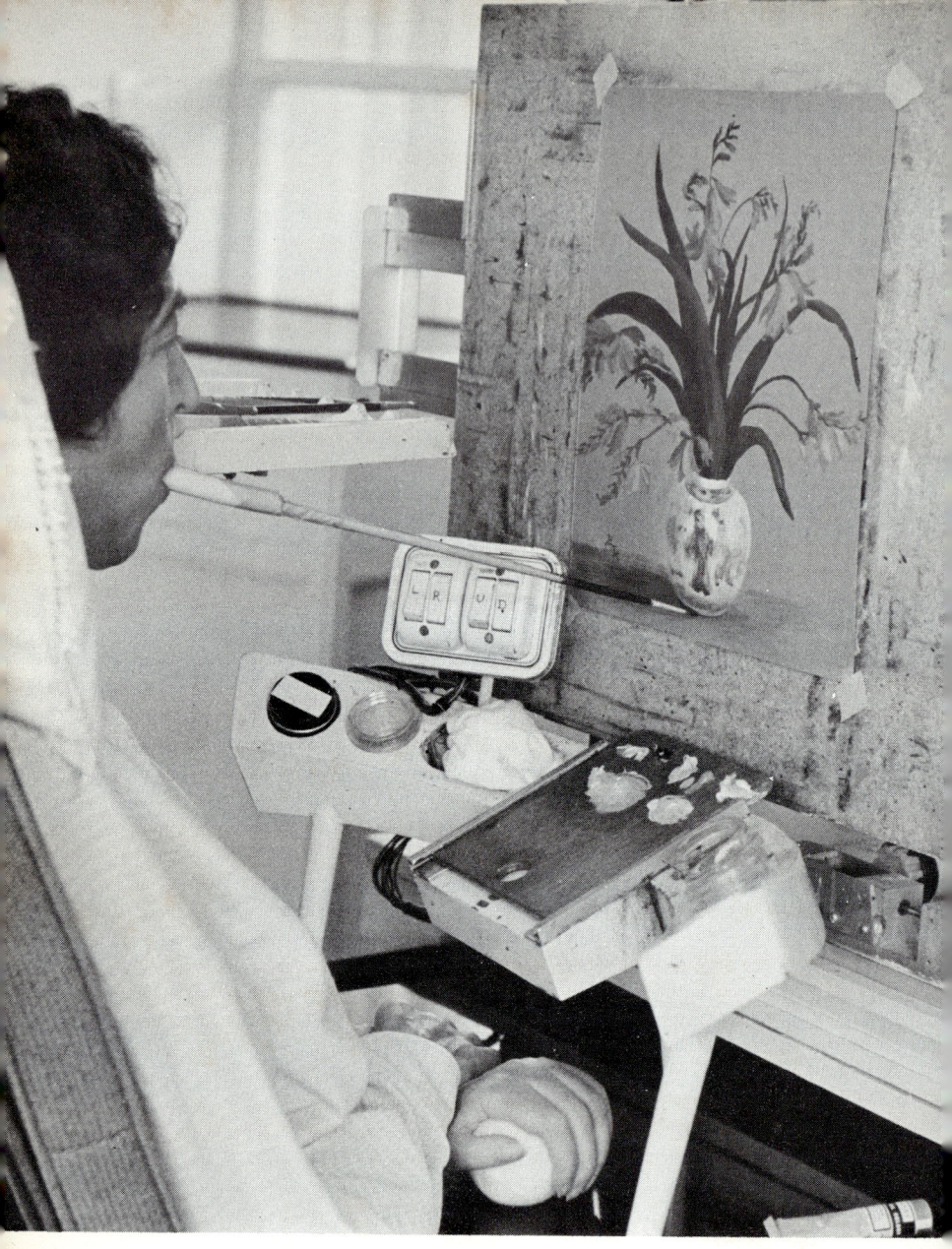

Painting   **NEM ELLIOTT**

The atmosphere in the theatre was tense. I was acutely aware that everyone was willing me to give of my best. Everywhere I looked, there were stage hands at the ready; I saw oxygen in the wings in case of emergency, but no guests.

I was pushed into position on the stage behind a table bearing microphones, a bowl of pink carnations and a whirring fan. The make-up girl stepped forward and powdered my face. My white pillow slips were changed for blue ones. As the programme was timed to the final second, Eamonn said he would prefer me to keep quiet! He was still talking to me as the signature tune started. I was quite unaware that there had been any warning—Eamonn disappeared through the curtains and we were on!

I heard him say, 'Tonight, "This is Your Life" is a birthday party, with birthday surprises for one of the most remarkable and courageous young ladies I have ever met.'

The curtains parted and I found myself facing a theatre full of people. I was back on stage!

As the applause died away, I heard the music of *Les Sylphides* and, on a monitor set, I saw some children dancing the Nocturne from this lovely ballet. They were pupils from the Cone School and were the first of my guests.

The others followed in quick succession: Jean Young, an Associate Member of the Royal Academy, recalled her memories of my dancing; Pat Dainton, one of my most talented and industrious pupils, remembered me as her teacher, as did Claire Bloom in a tele-recorded message from Hollywood.

The music of *Song of Norway* heralded the entrance of singers Janet Hamilton-Smith and John Hargreaves, followed by Pauline Grant, the choreographer for whom I worked so often; Charles Reardon, the stage doorkeeper, reviving happy memories of the time I spent at the Palace Theatre; the sound of squabbling off-stage, and the rushed entries of the Bernard Brothers dressed as Cinderella's ugly sisters—memories of the pantomime at the London Palladium.

Following my theatre colleagues, two children I used to teach at Coram's Fields. Then on to the present. Jenny and John Ripley; Rosemary Howard and one of her pupils who had modelled for me; Leslie Wilson, representing the Medici Galleries: David Blair and Beryl Grey from the Royal Ballet; my mother and father and finally, Margaret Roseby, also from the Royal Ballet, and her daughter. Eamonn presented me with the script and the curtain fell. The half hour had passed swiftly and pleasantly and I had enjoyed it after all.

This was the last I saw of Eamonn as he had to fly to Ireland immediately after the show. I felt slightly disappointed that he was unable to be with us, but suddenly, my sister Brighid and her husband were on the stage beside me. Unknown to me, they had been in the audience. They too were invited to the party held specially for all who had taken part in the programme. Here I met the production crew and was at last able to chat with my guests.

By eleven o'clock I was absolutely whacked. My thanks to everyone were completely inadequate—I was far too tired and breathless.

The R.M.O. greeted me on my return. He told me he had watched the programme with interest *and* with a degree of clinical concern. He could tell by the rapid movement of my neck muscles that I was exceedingly nervous, and that it took a good ten minutes for my respiration rate to return to normal.

The Houseman offered to help the nurses put me to bed. In spite of my exhaustion, his thoughtfulness amused and delighted me and I was quite disappointed when they said they could manage without him!

It was well after midnight before I was settled in my cuirass, but I was far too keyed up to sleep. The past few days had been such an emotional strain that it was to take nearly a week for me to unwind. Thoughts raced through my brain, and sleep, which is always elusive, escaped me altogether.

. . . . .

I returned to Dover Isolation Hospital two days later. Travelling in a hearse-like Daimler ambulance, I felt I was very much on view. All along the route, people recognised me; they stood up in the buses and along the streets, waving as I passed. I was staggered to think that my brief appearance on television had brought this publicity. The nurse beside me acknowledged these friendly greetings. She became quite tired waving continuously on my behalf, and said she wouldn't be the Queen for anything!

Gradually, I learned a little more about the preparations for the programme. I had not been the only one who had suffered agonies of nerves. My guests had been rehearsed for two days and had had to learn a script. Some of them were professionals and no doubt took it in their stride, but the others were unused to appearing in public and found it a terrible ordeal. Most of them were seeing me disabled for the first time and must have been shocked by what had happened to me. This must have added to their strain and I knew how I would have felt in their place. I think they were very plucky to appear in the show.

The most trying moment for me had been the appearance of my parents. I very nearly broke down. My heart ached with sympathy for them; I knew what it was costing them to stand up in public and make their speeches. By nature, they were reserved and retiring and, considering we had faced a live audience in the theatre as well as approximately fifteen million viewers, it was no wonder my poor mother got het up during rehearsals and felt she would never learn her lines. At one stage she even forgot which of her children she was talking about.

The producer, Leslie Jackson, a sensitive, very persuasive Irishman with several years' practice at overcoming people's diffidence and immediate reaction to a public appearance, must have had an awful time with my family. Whichever member he 'phoned, they all gave him the same answer, 'Good gracious!, you'll never get them to do that!'

I learnt later that my father told him he would walk round the garden until the show was over!

. . . . .

Life returned to normal and hundreds of letters poured in. My family helped me to answer them all. They came from all kinds of people—friends and complete strangers. I was glad to know that so many had enjoyed the programme, and I was very touched by the kind and gratifying things they wrote. My parents heard from people they had lost touch with more than forty years ago! A letter from one of my mother's first maids caused great amusement; she wrote, 'I don't know whether you'll remember me Madam, but I was the one who pushed Master Ian through the kitchen window!' Mother remembered this incident only too well.

My father heard from a soldier he had operated on in the first World War. The letter contained some of the medical notes in my father's handwriting which the man had 'pinched' from the foot of his bed.

Many people asked if they could buy my paintings, but I was unable to fulfil all the requests that were sent in.

We were thrilled and delighted to hear from so many people, and the odd, unpleasant letter found its way into the waste-paper basket.

There were a few cranky letters offering certain cures. Blackcurrant juice taken half-hourly and I would recover completely! I am afraid my faith did not stretch this far.

A few people wrote insinuating that my lack of recovery was due to a loss of faith. I think they are wrong! Accepting a disability is an *act* of faith—not a loss of faith. I have known other handicapped people who have received similar letters and been made utterly miserable by them.

As in all walks of life, opinions differ, and the disabled are no exception. A dramatic example of this occurred one day. I was talking to Mary and John, both badly paralysed as a result of polio. John and I agreed that it was God's will that we should get on and make the best of it. Mary reacted surprisingly and rebuked us with, 'You two have the Devil's own conceit to think in this way!'

John grinned (he had a wonderful sense of humour), but I was rather taken aback. We argued for a while and then asked her if she had a better suggestion. She said she was convinced that, if she prayed hard enough, she would gain complete recovery. I just could not understand this attitude. Despite tremendous advances in medical knowledge, no-one has yet found a cure for nerves destroyed by accident or disease. We were all so badly paralysed that only by a miracle could any of us walk again. By God's will, and through the dedicated skill and care by doctors and nurses, and untiring attention to our breathing machines by engineers, we had survived.

The dramatic first stage is followed by long, tedious months of waiting for the motor nerves to come back to life again and move our muscles. Long months of anxiety and disappointment; the gradual realization that, however hard you try, there is no response to the messages sent out by the brain. Frustration and despair build up inside as the terrible truth dawns; the future stretches endlessly before you—a life of immobility and utter helplessness.

Mary, John and I had had to face this upheaval and adjust ourselves to a new way of living. Our bodies felt no different; our brains worked the same, our thoughts, feelings and ambitions were unaltered. The only difference between us was our philosophy. John and I were trying to be realistic and face the medical facts; Mary was looking for something more. But, whatever the differences in our outlook and hopes for the future, we had a tremendous admiration for each other and have all had a measure of success in the paths we chose to follow.

There must be a story behind the life of every disabled person. That mine was chosen to be shown on television was for its visual appeal, and because it was easy for people to realise the enormous change from dancing on stage to a life of immobility in a wheelchair. There was no doubt at all that the public's imagination had been captured. Not only those leading a normal life, but disabled people too, known and unknown, wrote to me. The programme, they said, had been inspiring and encouraged them to new efforts. I was surprised and felt very humble. It had never occurred to me that my struggles to paint could have helped others in this way. It was one of the unexpected rewards. The other came a few weeks later. A special despatch rider drove up to the hospital with an enormous red morocco-bound book of photographs—a wonderful souvenir of an unusual and very happy birthday.

9

I GO TO SEA

AT times, I would get very restless and long to leap out of my wheelchair and go for a walk on my own. Lovely, open country is tantalising, spelling release and freedom to my restless spirit. Going for a walk in a wheelchair is poor compensation for the real thing, but life becomes so complex depending on other people, that modest desires such as this need forethought, and preparation. They tend to assume vast proportions in comparison with the request. Everyday activities are now impractical and sometimes impossible. Daily, you find yourself crushing the simplest desires most people are able to fulfil without thinking.

I am full of creative energy, formerly worked off in the ballet. Now this could only be satisfied by painting, typing or reading. But all these occupations involve gadgetry and a pair of willing hands to set me up. Now and again I am baulked by a person who is unco-operative and unsympathetic—occasionally even someone with slightly sadistic tendencies who seems to delight in the power they can wield.

I vividly recall one miserable visiting afternoon, when I spent an hour and a half looking at a blank wall because the nurses on duty were forbidden to set me up to read a book. To me, there seemed no reason why they could not have been allowed to spend the five minutes needed to set out my equipment. Obviously, if they had been busy I could have understood the refusal, but in this case, I felt it was pure victimization.

It is at times like this, when one is made to *really feel helpless*, disablement is hard to bear. Inwardly, I seethe with fury and explode in angry words—invariably adding fuel to the fire. This is stupidly rash of me, as I am completely at their mercy and it only antagonizes them further.

The patient satisfied with a cabbage-like existence is usually far more popular than the one with ambition and drive. So often, those in charge do not understand what lies behind this fighting spirit. To them, we appear difficult, demanding and an incredible nuisance. This battle against conflicting forces can easily wear you down and it takes a ruthless determination to reach the goal you set yourself. Fortunately, this obstructive type of person is in the minority and, in fifteen years, I have only crossed swords with a handful. Far more people understand my desire to work and my need to expend this energy in some creative activity.

Everywhere I have been, I have succeeded in getting through a small amount of work but not nearly enough to satisfy me. Institutional life is organised and restricting, the atmosphere one of perpetual bustle and 'bonhomie'. Regardless of the extent of your disabilities, you are expected to maintain a cheerful and placid disposition. Thoughtful silence is taken for moodiness; grumbles and complaints—lack of gratitude. You are expected to chat cheerfully and willingly to whoever passes your bed, and if you are trying to concentrate on your work, these distractions and interruptions can be infuriating.

My whole life consists of requests and explanations, which may have to be repeated many times. My shallow breathing makes this a tiring process and I am often unable to feel sociable. Though I enjoy meeting and talking to people, their visits sometimes leave me drained and exhausted—some days I cannot even muster the energy for conversation. Fortunately, most of my visitors realise this and understand.

I was beginning to feel that, if I was to succeed with my work, I must break away from the institutional atmosphere.

I must find a more congenial way of life—a home of my own with privacy and peace where I can be alone with my thoughts, where I can organise my day to suit myself and work for as long as I choose.

How would I set about gaining this freedom and independence I longed for? Obviously, the first step must be to get some form of transport—I must become more mobile.

When I was at Stanmore, the doctors had fitted me with a back splint which enabled me to be lifted out of my chair and into the front seat of an ordinary car. I was very awkward to handle in this way, and as I could not sit up for more than an hour at a time, I had to use the County ambulance for long journeys.

My father and I had lengthy discussions with a firm in Folkestone and eventually, a Bedford Utilicon, a gift from some very dear friends, was transformed into a small private ambulance especially designed to meet my needs. The roof was raised, and folding ramps were fitted at the rear so that I could be pushed aboard in my wheelchair and set down at my destination. A strong clamp anchors the wheelchair to the floor and I can either sit up or lie down while travelling. I have now been driven thousands of miles in this ambulance which has made an incredible difference to my life; making me independent in a way I had not thought possible, freeing me to go wherever I wished.

I wondered at first if I would find people to drive me. But there has always been a ready response—someone has always turned up. First on the scene was Ron, a member of the Deal Ambulance Service—cheerful, friendly, quick and efficient, and an excellent driver. He offered to look after my ambulance and drive me in his spare time. If he was on duty when I needed him, he would send a colleague.

Transport problems were now simplified and my next desire was to acquire a home of my own. I had spent nine years in hospital; it was time to get away and lead a more normal life. I began seriously to look at houses, flats and building sites, but it was to take two years before I found something suitable.

In 1962, I became a member of the Mouth and Foot Painting Artists Limited, which had been started in 1956 by a small group of severely disabled artists. The headquarters of this unique Association is in Liechtenstein, but exhibitions are held throughout the world and the membership is international, regardless of creed or colour.

If mouth or foot artists have achieved a certain standard they are invited to join. Their work is reproduced as greetings cards or calendars and sold to provide an income, which is distributed amongst the painters, giving them a regular salary so that they may work without undue financial strain. Even if a member is unable, for any reason, to continue painting, he still receives this salary.

When I first heard about the Association, it sounded too good to be true and it was some time before I could be persuaded to join. I did not want to abandon the contacts I had already made on my own in the art world, and there were long discussions about my contract as it meant that the Association would have the monopoly of my work. Eventually, it was agreed that some of my work could be used by other firms, but they must not mention that it was painted by mouth and the Association had to be kept informed.

I signed my contract and have never regretted my decision. It was the beginning of a more independent existence for me and it is greatly to the credit of Eric Stegmann—our President—that we disabled artists throughout the world can have such security.

He lost the use of his arms at the age of three as a result of polio, but with patience and determination, he learned to write and paint using his mouth. He became a first class artist with an international reputation and won many high awards, including the 'Lauro d'Oro Accademico' in Rome and the Silver Medal of the Academy of Arts and Science in Paris. He became a wealthy man but he was also a visionary and philanthropist, and the plight of other disabled artists was of real concern to him. With a view to helping those less fortunate than himself, he founded the Association of Mouth and Foot Painting Artists.

I still exhibited at the local art shows at Canterbury, Folkestone and Deal but now, through the Association, my work travelled to the far corners of the earth. Christmas card sales ran into millions and I received letters from all over the world. Letters of appreciation from unknown admirers, congratulations from colleagues and friends, and exclamations of pleasure from nurses who had cared for me in the early stages of my illness and who had now returned to their homes in Australia, New Zealand, Canada and America. It was encouraging and exciting to know that my work reached so many people.

All this could only have been achieved by the assistance of the nursing staff and members of the Dover Red Cross who came to the hospital regularly to help me. Each day, they set out my equipment for painting or typing, addressed envelopes, cut paper and packed up paintings for the post. They never counted the hours they gave me and never minded what I asked them to do. Rosemary prepared canvasses and mounted pictures for me and her husband lengthened my brushes. The nurses, poor things, had the mucky job of cleaning my palette and paint brushes after an art session. Painting is always a messy business, and I was well aware that I had the fun while others had all the drudgery. Their help was invaluable and without it I could have done nothing.

Summertime was lovely on the hilltop in Dover, but the dark, cheerless winter days dragged slowly by. Nineteen sixty-four seemed especially depressing, and one afternoon in February, as I flicked over the pages of a magazine, I saw an advertisement for a cruise to the sun on a Cunard liner. It sounded heavenly.

When Dr. Lynch did his afternoon round, I asked if it would be possible for me to go to sea. He assured me that it would, and that there was always a plentiful supply of electricity on board ship. There had been threatened power cuts up and down the country for several days, and he jokingly suggested that I should spend every winter at sea.

I took this to mean permission granted and wrote to a great friend of mine who had captained all the great Cunard liners. I had expected his reply to read 'what a lovely idea but, of course, it would be very difficult in a wheelchair' followed by various excuses. Instead of that, he wrote most enthusiastically, and immediately set the wheels in motion by writing to the company's Medical Superintendent, Dr. Heggie. Within a few days, this charming, forthright Scot travelled all the way from Liverpool to see me. He discussed the many problems with Dr. Lynch and my parents who had decided to come with me, and quickly determined that a voyage was possible.

The most suitable one was the twenty-day Mediterranean cruise on the *Mauretania*. The cabins on this liner were air-conditioned which would make life more comfortable should the climate be hot and humid.

Dr. Heggie rapidly assessed how much equipment I would need. He told me to take two respirators, one operating from the main electricity supply, the other from a twelve-volt battery, a Beaverometer also working from a battery, and a complete set of spare parts for all these machines. Everything was discussed with great care and every possible emergency anticipated. I was excused my T.A.B. injections on condition that I promised not to eat and drink when ashore. I was told there would be two doctors and three nursing sisters on board, but was asked if I could be independently nursed. The cruise was a large one and the medical staff would probably be kept very busy.

We all felt a bit dazed when Dr. Heggie left us. With stunning swiftness, he had smoothed out all our worries and problems and left orders for us to go ahead with the final arrangements.

Preparations started in earnest. Photographs and the exact measurements of my wheelchair were sent to the ship and to the International Red Cross headquarters in London. From there, letters were sent to each country we were to visit, asking if they could supply suitable transport for me. All the replies were favourable except from Tangier, where there was as yet no Red Cross. There were complications over my passport as I could not sign it myself. Numerous letters of explanation, and a visit to London on my behalf by the Commandant of the Dover Red Cross, eventually solved the problem.

My father dealt with the tickets and the money. I was feeling rather guilty about the expense but some generous friends offered help. My sister Alison and Janet Harvey[1] undertook to look after me. Gradually, all my equipment was accumulated, overhauled and tested and the spare parts packed and labelled.

A week before we were due to sail, my mother developed a septic finger. My father was extremely worried, but at the last moment, Dr. Boulden decided that she would be fit enough to travel with us.

I had orders from Cunards to be at the quayside promptly at two p.m. As it was a six-hour drive to Southampton, the night nurse had to call me at five-thirty a.m. Ron took half an hour to load my luggage and equipment into the ambulance, and we left Dover at eight o'clock in pouring rain. Janet had spent the night at the hospital and travelled with

[1] A friend who is a State Registered Nurse.

me. We had permission to drive right up to the ship's gangway, and arrived at exactly one minute past two.

Dr. Heggie and the ship's permanent Medical Officer were there to greet me. The pale green *Mauretania*, dressed over all, soared above me. Passengers were already boarding her from a nearby train and in spite of drizzling rain, there was a festive, holiday feeling in the air. I had expected to go through customs formalities, but quite suddenly, I was surrounded by an army of waiters and stewards. My luggage miraculously disappeared into the ship and my chair was gently lifted up the gangway and I found myself on board.

Janet and I squeezed into a minute lift that took us up to 'A' deck. The authorities had placed us as near to the centre of the ship as possible. Here there would be less movement should the sea be rough. We shared a large cabin, bathroom, shower and toilet, and had a communicating door through to my parent's suite. A special A.C. cable had been fitted for my respirator, as the rest of the electricity supply was D.C. The engineers were on a red light call system in case of emergencies and within minutes of my arrival, I was being introduced to the Chief Engineer. He said he would return when we had sailed to have a thorough look at all my machinery.

The cabin looked like a florist's shop and our stewardess kept bringing in more bouquets and telegrams. Strange, new faces kept appearing. I was introduced to representatives of the Cunard shore staff, the members of the crew, and to friends of the family whom I had never met before. Many had travelled a long way to wish us a 'bon voyage', and I was most touched that Dr. Lynch and his wife came to make sure that all was well.

When our visitors eventually left us, we went up on to the sun deck to watch the departure. With sirens hooting, the Mauretania was gradually eased away from the quayside by fussy little tugs. Gently we slipped down the Solent, passing the *Canberra*, the *Queen Mary* and many other big liners. The rain had stopped and the sun was shining.

When we got back to the cabin, the engineers were already examining the workings of my respirator motor. They were surprised at the simplicity of the machine, and I was most impressed by their enthusiastic thoroughness.

The carpenters came in and lashed everything movable to the walls of the cabin, and a steward battened down the porthole. Rough weather was expected. The doctors and nursing staff visited us, making sure we had everything we needed. It had been a long and very exciting day and we decided to have an early night.

Janet and Alison put me into my respirator, but when we switched on the motor we fused the electricity. As soon as we rang the bell, an engineer in spotless white uniform came and mended it. We tried again. The same thing happened! The cable was carrying a heavier load than had been anticipated. Soon, however, all was well and we were on our way towards the open sea.

A gale blew up in the night and the ship started to roll. I was too excited to sleep and the strange feeling of being rocked from side to side, and the weird creaking noises only added to the difficulty. We travelled miles off course to dodge the worst of the weather, but there was still a heavy sea running next morning and many of the passengers were seasick. Alison was one of the sufferers, so one of the nurses helped Janet to sit me in my wheelchair. I felt better sitting upright facing the porthole. It was rather like being on a rocking bed. My diaphragm obeyed the motion of the ship, which unfortunately was on the slow side for comfortable breathing. I for one would be glad when the rough weather was over.

My mother still had her arm in a sling and stayed in bed for safety. It was just as well she did, because at lunch time, an exceptionally big wave hit us broadside on. Everything was flung to the floor and there was a sound of crashing china all over the ship. My father hit the deck in the smoking-room and received a badly bruised shoulder, and there were several other minor casualties. We learnt that this wave was probably the result of an earthquake in some remote part of the world. It seemed a bad start to our cruise. I spent the entire day in the cabin—no-one could have pushed me along the corridor and it certainly would not have been safe to go up on deck.

Next day was completely different. The sea was calm, the sunshine glorious. We were passing the coast of Portugal and everyone was sunbathing on deck. It began to feel more like a holiday.

Meal times were leisurely affairs. There was an enormous choice of dishes and one could choose virtually anything one desired. The chefs accepted every challenge and took a great delight in sending up their specialities. Our first lunch in the dining-room lasted for two hours! This was far too long for me and I decided in future to make do with a snack on deck.

We were due to arrive in Tangier on the following day. Some time during the afternoon, the Staff Captain told me that if the sea was calm enough I would travel ashore in my own launch. It was still a mystery how I would be put into this, but I was not unduly worried. Everything had gone smoothly so far and I was sure it would all be beautifully organised.

The P.M.O. joined us for tea on deck. We soon discovered that we had many mutual friends and I felt that I had known him for years. He showed me the launch—*Boxer*—in which I would be travelling and introduced me to her crew. He also arranged for the ship's physiotherapist to give my mother treatment on her hand.

At a cocktail party that evening, I met Captain Treasure

Two of my paintings

Working on the book with Jacqueline Basford PHOTO: MERLYN SEVERN

Jones for the first time. A handsome, friendly man with great natural charm, he was obviously popular with passengers and crew. I was very surprised when he told me he was doing his best to get me ashore on the following day. Obviously, a great deal of thought had gone into the arrangements made for my welfare and comfort during this cruise, but I had not realised these things were discussed at such a high level and were the direct concern of the Captain himself.

We dropped anchor at eight in the morning and immediately, launches started taking people ashore. I longed to dash up on deck and see Tangier for myself; it was terribly frustrating lying in my bunk, waiting to be washed and dressed. Through the porthole I could see a cloudless blue sky and knew that it was a glorious sunny day, but I felt completely ostracized from the excitement going on outside. It was one of the times I resented my helplessness and I was filled with an aching desire for a normal, active body. I wanted to be on deck with the others and share the thrill of seeing a new port and a new continent for the first time. I did not see it until eleven o'clock, when we made our way to Main deck. *Boxer* was tied alongside and, under the eyes of the Staff Captain, First Officer, Bosun and his Mate, four sailors gently lifted me and my chair into the launch. Both brakes were put firmly on and one of the sailors stood behind my chair and held it for greater security. The family and Janet joined me and *Boxer* was swung out on the davits and lowered on to the water. The mystery was solved. We had abandoned ship!

As we drew away from the *Mauretania*, we could see how lovely she looked, lying at anchor in the deep blue sea. The sun blazed down and it was like a hot, summer day in England. *Boxer* had a crew of four and on this first trip, the First Officer accompanied us. In no time at all, we were at the quayside and I was being lifted up a steep flight of stone steps. I found myself on African soil for the first time.

We were immediately surrounded by traders, but we wanted to see Tangier. We wended our way through the midst of them and found a taxi driven by Mohammed Ben Said. I was strapped into my back-splint and he willingly helped to lift me into the front seat. My chair was folded and loaded into the back and we drove off on a sight-seeing tour. This was my first glimpse of tropical vegetation. The palm trees growing along the waterfront in the pavements looked rather dead and uncared for, and the prickly pear, spelling romance to my imagination, was disappointing in reality. The trees of mimosa and bougainvillaea however, were at their best, making vivid splashes of colour against the white buildings and azure sky. Groups of smiling, dark haired children dressed in colourful shirts and dresses, stood barefoot by the wayside, selling flowers to the tourists. We could not resist their smiling faces and soon, the scent of mimosa filled the taxi.

Obviously, old traditions died hard in this town that was rapidly being modernized and there was a great variety of costumes to be seen. Women completely shrouded in gowns of black or brown, showing only their eyes to the public, and men in burnous and embroidered caps or red fezes. Contrasts between rich and poor, old and new were obvious even from a taxi.

The countryside beyond Tangier was rugged and wild. There seemed little pasture for the goats and mules tethered by the roadside and the animals looked terribly thin. It was hot and we were glad when Mohammed left us on a quiet beach overlooking the Mediterranean. Here, we ate our picnic lunch and Janet and Alison bathed.

Mohammed returned for us in the afternoon and as we passed a long queue of mothers and children, he told us they were getting their polio injections. When we arrived at the quayside, an Officer called the Bridge on a walkie-talkie, and

I GO TO SEA

summoned our launch for us. Again, the First Officer came with our crew and this time, took us for a trip round the harbour before returning to the ship. There was a stiff breeze blowing and the sea was rough. *Boxer* rocked considerably as she was hooked on to the chains and hoisted up on the davits. I must confess I was a bit frightened at this procedure and was glad to be in the safety of the *Mauretania* again. The doctor and Staff Captain were awaiting our return and seemed relieved that all had gone smoothly, and that we had all enjoyed our first trip ashore.

It was long after midnight before I was settled in my respirator, and I could not help comparing this with my early nights in hospital.

As we travelled along the north coast of Africa, it was a calm, hot day, but as we approached Malta the weather changed and the sea became very rough. Next morning, we anchored outside Valetta harbour. The landing was cancelled and only the mail boat was launched. It was tantalizing.

When I saw Captain Treasure Jones later that day, I asked him if it would be possible to call at Malta on the way back. He said that he would not promise anything but that he would telephone London and see what could be done. I thought he was just saying this to please me, but found out later I was quite mistaken.

The weather was altogether different the next morning when we all assembled for life-boat drill. This was the first combined practice for crew and passengers and the Captain explained exactly what would happen should we have to abandon ship. I think I was the only passenger who did not put on a life jacket. (It was the type that would have floated me face downwards anyway, so would have been of little use.) I had asked the doctor about it when I first came on board, and he told me not to worry, that he would jump in with me. When it came to the drill, however, he was nowhere to be seen. I asked him later where he had been hiding. 'Oh,' he said. 'I was on duty in the hospital'. This was on 'E' deck five decks below us!

On 1 April, we docked at Alexandria. Delegates from the Red Crescent (the Egyptian equivalent of the Red Cross) arrived on board. They gave me a vast bouquet of red and white gladioli and blue irises, and then we went ashore at about ten-thirty through an attractively modern customs hall and down in an enormous lift. Our escorts had provided excellent transport facilities and we formed quite a procession as we left the quayside. Mr Tarrahoney, who had once swum the English Channel, escorted Janet, Alison and myself in a small van which was just large enough for my wheelchair. My parents travelled with the chief delegate, Madame Said, driven by her chauffeur wearing black robes edged with gold and a red fez. A third car followed with the other members of the Red Crescent.

Our first visit was to the Aquarium of which they were very proud, but I felt it was a waste of time to have come all the way to Egypt to look at tropical fish that were better displayed in the London Zoo, and I was glad when we drove on to King Farouk's Palace at Ras el Tin. Here a guide awaited us and we spent some time in this fabulous but ostentatious home of Egypt's ex-king. Beautiful inlay work, magnificent chandeliers, huge mahogany doors and gold leaf everywhere. The bathroom was quite fantastic and it was easy for me to be wheeled round the bath in my wheelchair! It was a huge sunken bath but latterly, even this was too small for His Majesty. Such luxury was a great contrast to the appalling poverty elsewhere.

The Egyptian newspapers had reported my visit that morning, and as we wandered round the Mouzha Antoniades Gardens, some High School girls from Cairo came over and presented me with red roses. They were so sweet and it was a pity I could not talk to them in their own language. The afternoon became very hot, and we were very glad to return to the air-conditioned ship.

Next day, the representatives of the Red Crescent arrived with another enormous bouquet, this time mimosa and sweetpeas. We visited the Museum where I was interviewed by the Press. We then drove right through Alexandria to a private beach in the grounds of the Montazza Palace which had belonged to King Farouk. We had a picnic lunch by the water's edge under shady palm trees. It was quite heavenly.

In the afternoon, we were entertained by Madame Said in her beautiful home. Her picturesque chauffeur did services as butler and served us with tea and cakes. We met her two little grandchildren and were introduced to her husband, Mahmoud Said. He was a retired judge, son of an ex-prime minister and now one of Egypt's leading artists. I was able to see some of his paintings, mostly landscapes and portraits, executed in a bold and highly individual style. It was a delightful interlude and, as we left the house, Madame Said presented me with a book about her husband's work.

We had only a brief trip ashore on the following morning. Our Egyptian entourage had arrived with more flowers and we went to visit a mosque. Unfortunately, they had forgotten it was Friday and we were not able to go inside. We bought a national newspaper and discovered that there was half a page of photographs of our museum visit and a write-up in Arabic. We were due to sail at two p.m. so we returned to the ship for lunch. As I went up the gangway, an official stepped forward and presented me with a huge bowl of flowers, a gift from the immigration and customs Officers. It was a most touching gesture.

We had had an interesting and very enjoyable three days and my visit to Egypt had been flowers all the way.

We sailed north to Greece. I had been looking forward to

this visit as I was to meet again one of the doctors who had organised my first outing from the National Hospital, my return to Covent Garden eight years ago. She was now married and living with her husband and two children in a house on the outskirts of Athens. She had been in touch with the Greek Red Cross, who met me with a spacious ambulance into which my chair fitted beautifully.

The atmosphere was fantastically clear and when we stopped at various view points, we could see for miles. Of course, we visited the Acropolis, but it never entered my head that my friends would arrange for me to be carried up its steep sides and right round the Parthenon. They inveigled two members of the Greek Airforce to help and, between them, they did just this. Large boulders were strewn on the ground all around and it was almost impossible to find enough level ground on which to rest the chair. It was certainly an endurance test for my kindly porters, but they gave me one of the most memorable mornings of my life. This beautiful and impressive ruin rose majestically above me into the clear blue sky. Its superbly proportioned pillars soaring upwards like a song of praise. It was amazing to think it had been standing since the 5th century B.C. We had lunch on the terrace in the warm sunshine and in the afternoon, drove to Marathon through woods filled with spring flowers. We were told that the road we took back to Athens was the route of the original Marathon race, which is still commemorated yearly. Our Red Cross drivers are always there to help those that fall by the wayside!

We made a brief stop at Raphina Bay, a tiny fishing village whose main street is also the quayside. We arrived just as a group of fishing smacks sailed out from the harbour. Their snow-white sails and vivid red paintwork looked magnificent against the deep blue of the sea. I longed to have my paint brushes to hand, or should I say, to mouth. Our hosts offered us glasses of Retsina, the local wine, but as it was a very hot afternoon, we settled for something non-alcoholic. We had had a wonderful day and on my return to the ship, I found a lovely bouquet from the Greek Red Cross.

Everyone expected Gibraltar to be our next stop, but Captain Treasure Jones had had permission to travel two hundred miles off course so that we could call at Malta en route. We were all delighted. This time the sea was calm and we docked in Valetta harbour and went ashore in *Boxer*. Girls in national costume lined the quayside greeting the tourists with flower buttonholes.

We were met by two members of the Maltese Polio Fund and made a brief tour of Valetta in their ambulance. During this drive, my father had a severe fainting attack which was very worrying. Fortunately, it was quickly over and we went on to the San Anton Palace, the home of the Governor of Malta, Sir Maurice Dorman. He was away, but Lady Dorman was a charming hostess and gave us a great welcome. Drinks were served under a tulip tree in the garden in the warm sunshine. She had arranged a very pleasant surprise for me. My specialist from Stanmore, Sir Harry Seddon, happened to be on the island at the same time and Lady Dorman had very kindly invited him and his wife along too. It was eleven years since we had met and he aptly remarked, 'We could meet in England, Elizabeth. We shouldn't need to come all this way!'

We were then taken to Medina, the old capital of Malta, for lunch at the Xara Palace Hotel. There, I gave a Press interview and we were photographed once again. Unfortunately, we had to rush back to the ship and did not do justice to the delicious local dishes and wine they had provided for us. This was the second time I had broken my promise to the doctor and eaten on shore, fortunately with no ill results. It was a very hurried drive back to the docks and we left

Malta most reluctantly. It had been a marvellous visit and I hoped sincerely that I would be able to return one day.

We spent the following day quietly resting on deck and made a brief inspection tour of the galleys. It was fascinating to see the organisation that went on behind the scenes in this spotlessly clean, though intolerably hot, kitchen. It was a most interesting visit and we were able to thank the chefs personally for the wonderful menus they had served us.

In Gibraltar we were met by the Red Cross with a Royal Naval patrol car, driven by two Military Policemen. They assured us that, showing us the Rock made a change from picking up intoxicated sailors.

Next day, we anchored in the Tagus and had a look at the beautiful city of Lisbon. We had a wonderful day ashore, travelling miles in 'Grandfather's old Daimler'. This grand old car was supplied by the Portuguese Red Cross and our escort was a medical student, a bull fighter in his spare time! I had had to sit all day in my back-splint, which was anything but comfortable, and I was utterly exhausted. This visit to Portugal had been tantalisingly brief and I longed to see more of this lovely country.

The end of the cruise was sad and somewhat depressing, rather like the end of a party. It was livened by the children's fancy dress parade and a special ballet recital given to me by two little girls, who, in spite of a rolling ship, danced splendidly; and one evening, in my cabin, I found a sailor's cap autographed by the Bosun and many of the crew, a unique favour of which I am very proud.

The sea got rougher and the weather colder as we returned to England. We had made many friends during the last three weeks and even the Captain came to my cabin to say goodbye. Customs officials came, followed by Ron with the ambulance. We drove back to Dover.

I GO TO SEA

The countryside looked beautiful in the spring sunshine, and in spite of all the sad farewells, it was good to be home again.

. . . . .

I was re-admitted to the Isolation Hospital and my days of living it up were over. Life returned to normal.

I had travelled nearly 9,000 nautical miles and it had been a great adventure. The nurses thought I looked well, but I knew I needed a rest after the late nights and continuous excitement of the cruise.

Soon, I was back to work and started to get some paintings ready for another one-man show at the Dover Public Library. Rosemary again helped me to prepare my work but this time, my pictures overflowed the glass case in the hall and were hung up the stairs and in the windows overlooking the street. I made a brief appearance on television and the local press gave me useful publicity. From the sales angle, this was a successful show, but I also had one of my paintings stolen. Someone cut it off the wall. Goya's portrait of the Duke of Wellington was stolen from the National Portrait Gallery at about the same time, so I felt I was in good company.

My father had never been a very robust man and had suffered a minor heart ailment for many years. He began to look very frail and it was obvious he would have to take life more easily. When I planned to go on another cruise, he decided that he did not feel fit enough to accompany me.

I was joining the *Mauretania's* final trip round the Mediterranean before she went to the scrap heap at the end of the year. We were to travel as far east as Israel and the Lebanon and as far north as Naples, and make return visits to Tangier, Malta and Gibraltar. Israel insisted on certificates of vaccination against smallpox, but I was excused this on medical grounds. Instead, I took a letter of explanation from Dr.

Lynch. On my return to England, however, I was kept under observation for three weeks.

Janet Harvey and Sheila Forster, who had looked after me in London, were coming with me and preparations began for my second journey. Again I contacted the International Red Cross. This time, all the replies were favourable, and there was promise of suitable transport everywhere. Both the doctors on board would be new to me and visited me in Dover so that they could become acquainted with me and my equipment before we set out on the trip.

A few weeks before I sailed, my father heard of a ground floor flat for sale in Walmer. It sounded ideal and we went to see it. I liked it immediately and within forty-eight hours it was mine. This lightning decision was quite unlike the family's usual cautious behaviour. I know that if the flat had come on the market sooner, I would not have planned a second luxurious holiday.

We boarded the *Mauretania* at Southampton on April 10th, receiving a great welcome from many old friends. We had the same communicating cabins and my A.C. cable was still in place. Our stewardess, who for the past few months had been working on Main deck, had asked if she could return to 'A' deck especially to look after us. Her devotion was most touching and we were delighted to see her again. My cabin was soon full of flowers and again, we had a wonderful send off.

For the first two days we travelled through the Bay of Biscay, which was much calmer than last year. I was looking forward to my return visit to Tangier, but as we travelled ashore in *Boxer*, I had no idea just how different this visit was going to be. Last year, there had been no Red Cross in Morocco. Now there was the Red Crescent, backed by the Americans, and their idea of hospitality left little to be desired. My first intimation that this was going to be a fantastic day came as I arrived on the quayside. Someone said to me, 'The Governor of Morocco is coming to visit you.'

I felt sure this remark should have been addressed to someone else and I just laughed. I meant no disrespect but it sounded so incredible! There was already a deputation from the Red Crescent awaiting our arrival headed by Mr. Boucherine, the President—by profession a High Court judge. They spoke only French and Arabic but had brought an American as interpreter. Sheila spoke fluent French, so communications were not too difficult. They had with them the perfect vehicle, lent by Voice of America, and I was lifted into it in my chair and anchored securely with ropes. We set off on a sight-seeing tour through Tangier towards Cape Spartel, the most north-westerly point of the African continent, where giant rolling waves crashed on to long stretches of sandy beach. En route, we stopped to watch a group of men and boys performing traditional dances. On the drive back to the city, we saw some camels—including one only eighteen days old, a most endearing little animal.

We stopped for drinks at a café which we had in the garden in the hot sunshine, then drove back to Mr. Boucherine's house for lunch. This turned out to be a banquet in my honour. The guest list was most impressive and included the Vice President of the Moroccan Red Crescent wearing traditional dress, the British Consul and his wife, the American Consul and his wife, the American Vice Consul and his wife, an American Diplomat and his wife; representatives of The Voice of America, two Spanish doctors and their wives and another High Court judge. Sheila and these very eminent guests sat in the main reception room on leather pouffes circling low, round tables, while Janet and I were set apart in a small alcove but so placed that we could watch all that went on. Mr. Boucherine himself supervised the proceedings in the kitchen, while a friend of his organised everything in the dining room. The meal was served to us by a small, barefooted maid wearing a brightly coloured dress and pinafore and a red spotted handkerchief round her head. It was very picturesque—the kind of setting one only reads about in books.

I felt I was being rather disrespectful to my host by not partaking of his magnificent meal. Indeed, I was so conscious of my bad manners that I could hardly eat any of the chicken sandwiches that the ship's chef had made for me. I only hope he understood and forgave me, for as I watched the meal progress and saw one rich course follow another, I realised that Dr. Heggie's order that I should eat nothing ashore was a very wise one.

Everyone ate with their fingers, which was rather tricky for those unused to doing so. The meal started off with enormous flat pies, about sixteen inches in diameter. They were made of flaky pastry filled with chicken, eggs, spices and herbs. One tore off a slice single-handed, and dipped it in icing sugar. Poor Janet had a whole one to herself and made little impression on it. The next course was Shish-Kebabs (sheep's livers stuck on skewers cooked over charcoal) and large oval-shaped loaves of white bread served from coloured baskets into which the fragments were collected afterwards. Then came chicken cooked in oil, garlic, spices and olives, and once again, Janet was faced with a whole one. She said it was delicious but it looked frightfully rich to me. I warned her not to eat too much as I felt sure there would be more to come. There was! Mutton, cooked in oil and curry and festooned with almonds and prunes. This was followed by fresh fruit and glasses of drinking water handed round in gold holders.

Everyone then moved to the seats round the sides of the room and began smoking. The little maid went round with a ewer and basin, pouring water over the guests' hands and drying them on a towel. Glasses of mint tea were served. This is quite a ritual and is made in front of all the guests.

I GO TO SEA

Mr. Boucherine's friend knelt on the floor in front of a large silver tray. He crammed mint and lumps of rock sugar into a beautiful silver teapot and filled it up with boiling water. I tasted some of this and found it quite delicious.

After this stupendous meal, I met and talked to the various guests. Many of them thanked *me* for coming and I was very surprised when they said that it was the first time they had been invited to such a banquet. I suddenly realised that I had been paid the very highest possible compliment, and felt touched and very honoured.

I was told that there was to be another reception for me at the Sultan's palace in the afternoon, but before setting out for this, it was necessary for me to retire to the 'Ladies'. Sheila asked Mr. Boucherine about the matter and he took her up three flights of spiral staircase! She said it would be impossible to get me up there in my chair, so he showed her into a minute bathroom on the ground floor. With careful manipulation, we squeezed the chair in. Janet stood in the bath, Sheila put a foot on the bidet and, with much hilarity, we managed to cope.

We then set off for the Sultan's palace, driving through the Kasbah, which was closed for the three-day Easter sheep-killing holiday. The palace had been built and given to a Sultan when he retired and, on his death, it was purchased by the Italian Government as a school for Science and Technology. It was also used for large receptions and had been lent to the Red Crescent for the afternoon. The ceilings and upper walls were of carved wood and were painted in vivid colours. The lower walls were of mosaic. The garden, surrounded by cloisters, was filled with oranges, a type of red lily, and many other tropical plants—an exotic setting enhanced by the presence of a couple of vivid blue peacocks.

I was pushed into the main reception hall, where one of

Tangier's leading artists had hung some paintings for my inspection. Against the ornate, highly coloured walls of this beautifully proportioned room, his work did not show to its best advantage. But it was an interesting little collection and I loved his impasto landscapes, showing the warmth of the Moroccan sun and the lush tropical vegetation. It was a thoughtful gesture, and I was delighted to meet the artist himself.

About a hundred guests had been invited to the reception and they gradually assembled. Many of the women were closely veiled but I noticed that the yashmaks were removed for photographs. I was introduced to many of them, smiled, nodded and chatted in English. They replied in Arabic or French. Though our conversation was limited, the atmosphere was very friendly and our interpreters had a busy afternoon.

A Moroccan band, thirteen strong, arrived. They played with gusto; in fact, we found the music rather too loud for comfortable conversation. We were told that, when they heard of our visit to Tangier they offered their services free, even though it was their feast day. The music was lively and very exciting, and through our interpreters, we tried to convey how much we had enjoyed it.

Mint tea and cookies were served while we awaited the arrival of the Governor. Soon after six o'clock, however, we received a message from him to say that he was exhausted and would not be able to keep his appointment. This was very disappointing, but understandable because he had recently been ill. I was getting pretty exhausted myself by now, so after talking to the Press and having our photographs taken, we left our guests and returned to the quayside.

Our arrival there coincided with *Boxer's* (royal timing) and after fond farewells to our kindly hosts, we sailed back to the *Mauretania*.

I had been treated like a princess and felt sure that no other passenger could have spent the day as I had. Looking back on it, it all seemed completely unreal, but it had been a wonderful day and one that I would never forget.

We sailed from Africa that evening, travelling north to Naples where we were to stay for thirty-six hours. The ambulance belonging to the Italian Red Cross had opaque windows and was not very good for sight-seeing. We drove to Pompeii and joined the crowds visiting the ruins. Unfortunately, there were too many steps and the ground was too steep and uneven for my wheelchair, so we only visited the House of Misteri. This was fascinating and helped to allay the disappointment of not seeing the whole site.

The House of Misteri is a large Roman Villa containing some extremely well-preserved murals. As I was pushed round, it was not hard to imagine life as it had been in this prosperous seaside resort before the historic eruption of Mount Vesuvius in AD 79. Here were the partly opened window shutters, the pottery, the furniture, the cooking utensils and the food. Here were the people who had been using these everyday objects, now petrified mummies still lying as they had fallen, their faces and attitudes portraying forever that horrifying moment in time when a wall of boiling lava had entombed them. These carefully preserved remains brought this tragedy of long years ago vividly to life, and I was glad to get back into the bright Italian sunshine and leave that house of sadness and horror behind. Vesuvius rose above us, majestic and peaceful as we took the road through the towns of Pompeii and Salerno, to Maiori for a picnic lunch on the beach.

We returned to Naples in the afternoon following the beautiful coast road, stopping now and again to admire the view. By the time we got back to the ship, we had travelled over two hundred kilometres and felt pleasantly weary.

The second day in Italy was spent looking round Naples. Our escorts concentrated on the prosperous parts of the city, but we would have liked to explore the back streets—the less salubrious but more picturesque parts of the port.

We made an early return to the ship, and later that night, we left for the Lebanon. We were to be two days at sea and these were bright and sunny and we spent a restful time on deck. Passengers were kind, friendly and hospitable and cocktail parties were a daily, sometimes twice daily, occurrence. Menus were fantastic and the chefs took a great delight in thinking up new and original meals especially for us. All the food was delicious but our waiters were constantly asking us if there was some speciality we would like.

One evening I had fruit salad with a dash of Kirsche on it. When I mentioned that I liked Kirsche, I got it on everything for the next few nights, until I had to ask them to leave it off! Such was their desire to please.

When we docked in Beirut, there were dark thunder clouds towering over the port and it looked as though it would rain. Fortunately, these lifted and the day became very warm. There had been some misunderstanding here regarding our transport and the Lebanese Red Cross had failed to send an ambulance. Sheila tried to sort things out on the telephone, but we decided to take a taxi and go up to the Red Cross office. Everyone there was most apologetic, friendly and helpful. We had decided to spend a lazy day on the beach and were told the nicest one to visit. It was a bit of a struggle to get my wheelchair over the sand, but with some assistance from the beach attendant, we settled ourselves under a gay canvas awning. The sun got very warm but there was a cold wind blowing and, though the sea looked tempting, Janet and Sheila said it was too rough to bathe.

The Red Cross sent an ambulance to fetch us, and before returning to the ship, we drove round Beirut and had a look at the airport. I imagine that the most interesting part of the Lebanon to see is further inland, but as this would have involved a sharp rise in altitude (which would have affected my breathing) it would not have been wise to attempt it in a single day.

Very early the following morning, we docked at Haifa and representatives of the Star of David, the Israeli Red Cross, called at our cabin to ask what we would like to do. We said we would like to see as much of Israel as possible and promised to be ready to leave the ship soon after nine o'clock. They returned with a journalist, a photographer, an excellent ambulance and an enormous bouquet of pink roses. We drove to Ein Hod, one of Israel's flourishing art colonies. Painters, sculptors and craftsmen lived on this hillside overlooking the sea with a distant view of a lovely old castle dating back to the time of the Crusades. Each had his own house and studio, and exhibited their work in a magnificent modern art gallery. We were shown round this by the Directress who spoke excellent English. She introduced us to many of the artists, including Gertrude Krause, Israel's leading dance choreographer who had turned her talents to painting, and Peter Jochanny, who worked in silver and had some of his work permanently on view at the Victoria and Albert Museum in London. Gertrude was a petite, lively person with straight, dark hair. We had no trouble at all understanding each other, thanks to Gertrude's expressive miming. Peter Jochanny was a modest, gentle-looking man who, I imagine, had seen much suffering in life. I was most touched when he went off to his garden to gather me some sweetpeas. I felt it had been a great privilege meeting these delightful artists and seeing how and where they worked.

We drove over Mount Carmel along a narrow, bumpy road, rugged, uninhabited country on either side. The views were wonderful—wild flowers growing in great profusion, making brilliant splashes of red and yellow, white and blue. We stopped for lunch in Nazareth, a town I would like to explore on foot. It was a busy, bustling place full of contrasts —new buildings rapidly rising beside the old ones and flocks of sheep and goats vying with the traffic of today. We ate our sandwiches at a very modern hotel, cool and peaceful set back from the busy, jostling high street. The 'Ladies' room here was down a very steep flight of stairs. I took one look at them and felt petrified. I was not given time to refuse the descent, however; the Manager had already called four waiters. None of them spoke English, but they immediately seized my chair, and with a great deal of shouting and gesticulating carried me safely to the bottom.

In the afternoon, we drove through Cana and Tiberius down to the Sea of Galilee. This is 682 feet below sea level and I got rather breathless and scared. My chest felt as though it had a heavy weight on it and for one awful moment, I thought I would not be able to continue the tour. It took me about half an hour to become acclimatised.

The Sea of Galilee was as I had always imagined it—a brilliant blue, surrounded by reddish-tinged hills. We drove along the shore to the south and saw where the River Jordan flows out of it—vividly green. We passed people water ski-ing and bathing and, in complete contrast, fishermen in little boats looking as they must have done in the time of Our Lord. It was peaceful and very beautiful.

We were taken to see the Afikin Kibbutz and on our way there, passed groves of bananas. We were met at the entrance by the Director who gave us special permission to drive slowly round the grounds. Here we learnt something of life in a kibbutz. There were houses for each age group set in their own gardens. Babies and small children were cared for by professional nurses, which had cut down infant mortality to a minimum. The parents of these children were thus free to do a full day's work within the community and were able to spend approximately four hours each evening with them. The Israelis felt that, in this way, their children saw more of their parents than ours. Western parents were often working all day and had to spend the evening catching up on the housework. No-one is compelled to live in a kibbutz but, if they did, they worked as a community. They had no need of money as everything was provided for them in return for their services. Personally, I would not like to live in this way; but then I had never been a stateless person entering a new country with nothing to my name, and in Israel it seems to work well.

We drove along the west coast of the Sea of Galilee to the northern-most end. Here I met and talked to the Director of another kibbutz—a charming old man, who told me that he and his generation had been worried that the youngsters would leave the Kibbutzim and live elsewhere. He was obviously delighted that many had recently returned to carry on the work that their elders had pioneered. He told me what an uphill job it had been to make the soil of Israel produce enough food. Much of it was swampland and had had to be drained and malaria, which was rife when he first came, was now a disease of the past. It seemed to me that everyone worked exceedingly hard and that they were doing a magnificent job.

It was a long drive back to Haifa and the *Mauretania*, and I was very tired, but it had been a most interesting and instructive day.

We made an early start the next morning and drove up Mount Carmel, from the top of which we had a magnificent view of Haifa. We spent some time at a flower show and then took a long drive inland to a village called Assafia. This was one of about eighteen villages occupied by Druses, who are a small sect having their own unique way of life and practising a secret, mystical religion. Life in this village was obviously rather primitive. The road was little more than a track and there were only a handful of houses, and a few stores whose goods were displayed on the roadside. It was extremely hot as we got out of the ambulance to do some shopping, and we were quickly surrounded by dozens of small girls. They were full of curiosity and came with us into the first shop which was full of rather dusty souvenirs. Sheila had decided that she wanted a tall basket with a lid, but our escorts told us the salesman here was charging about fifty per cent too much, and after much arguing and bargaining, we all moved further on up the village to a more prosperous-looking store. Here, Sheila was successful and managed to buy a basket at a fair price and we left the village for Caesaria.

We passed groves of olives and oranges and saw acres of lovely wild flowers. We were driven to an exceedingly grand hotel—the 'Dorchester' of Israel—built with money given by Baron Rothschild. Designed by a Frenchman and built entirely of material produced in Israel, it was so spacious that it felt empty as I was pushed along wide corridors, through glass doors, up an enormous lift, and on to the terrace overlooking the swimming pool and the only golf course in the country.

There were very few visitors and we felt rather embarrassed eating our picnic lunch under the eyes of some very efficient-looking waiters. Soon the hostess appeared, an attractive, charming ex-ballet teacher. She quickly put us at our ease and said how delighted she was to extend to us the facilities of the hotel. We had a most interesting talk and she gave us some pieces of old Roman pottery which she had picked up locally on the site of an amphitheatre which had recently been excavated and completely renovated. It was now used for concerts, ballet and drama performances. We left her most reluctantly and drove back along the main road to Haifa, and later that afternoon, set sail for Malta.

In the evening, there was a piano recital by Rawitz and Landaur, who very kindly played a Chopin Waltz especially for me. Next day, the officers gave a cocktail party for Janet, Sheila and myself, to which the Captain, Staff Captain, Walter Landaur and Captain 'Corpus' Jones (ex-Captain of the *Queen Elizabeth*) were also invited. It was a very jolly party and the First Officer gave us each a sailor doll as a memento. In the evening, we went to the Chief Engineer's party, and later still, were entertained by one of the doctors. It was all rather exhausting and we felt that a trip ashore would be quite a welcome rest!

I was very excited at seeing Malta again. The same welcoming party were on the quayside to greet us, but they were going to a wedding and our tour this year was in the hands of a Countess. After a brief chat, I was loaded into the ambulance, and we left Valetta and drove round the coast to Delimara and on to Mu'hokk, a fishing village with lots of brilliantly coloured boats at anchor in the bay. We passed through many interesting villages and went on to Zurried, where the Countess had her country palace.

The Countess was typically Maltese, dark, plump and very jolly with flashing black eyes and an infectious laugh. She fished around in her large black bag and brought out an enormous old-fashioned key, with which she opened her front door. This large house, built by the Grand Masters, was full of beautifully proportioned rooms with graceful arches over huge double doors and floors colourfully tiled. There was an attractive garden at the back, where the Countess and her gardener picked oranges, lemons and mint for us and we had a brief tour round it all. The Countess was obviously very popular and many of the local people waved to her and called greetings to us as we left.

We only had time to visit the temples of the Goddess of Fertility, built in 2000 BC, before dashing back to the quayside. On the way, however, we stopped to buy some Maltese cheese cakes for the *Boxer* crew. They smelt delicious and were very popular. As before, our visit had been all too brief, but we had enjoyed it nonetheless.

The next day was wet and cold, and there were intermittent hail showers. There was a fast sea running and Sheila was a bit under the weather with sea sickness. We watched the children's fancy dress party in the afternoon, then dressed and went down for dinner. The passengers at the next table were celebrating a birthday and there was cake and champagne for us as well. When our stewardess came to visit us before going off duty, she was rather horrified to find us all flat out, too tired to get down to the job of putting me to bed!

There was brilliant sunshine but a very stiff breeze blowing as we approached the Rock of Gibralter. This was to be our last port of call, and again, we hoped to meet some of the people we had met last year. It was too rough for us to travel in *Boxer*, so we went ashore on the 1.30 p.m. tender. Last year, it had been extremely difficult for me to disembark from this, so Captain Treasure Jones said that he would see what other arrangements could be made. He sent the Second Officer ashore with us, who organised things superbly, and unloaded me directly on to the quayside from the top deck of the tender.

A Lieutenant Commander from Deal greeted us on our arrival, together with a naval patrol car and a crew of three Petty Officers. With them, was one of the Red Cross representatives who had met us last year. We were delighted to see her again and it was a great reunion. The boys, Clive, Rex and George, had been detailed to take care of us, and we were each given a typed route and schedule for our day's outing. I was lifted into the car and fixed securely with a

I GO TO SEA

'two-screw' job, which they considered one up on last year's rope! A little coloured sunshade had also been provided and was kept adjusted by Clive so that my head was always in the shade.

Our first stop was the airfield, where we were met by the Commander-in-Chief, who then handed us over to his Flight Lieutenant, an amusing character. He took us to see his beloved Shackletons; he was devoted to these aircraft because he could get a three-course meal on board! We had a lecture tour of the airport which we thoroughly enjoyed, and watched some jets landing and taking off—and overshooting the runway.

When we left, we drove up the Rock to see the Apes, stopping en route to admire the wonderful view and to acclimatise me gradually to the change of altitude. We stopped twice between six hundred and eight hundred feet and I found I very quickly adjusted my breathing. There was a long queue of cars at the top, which was immediately dispersed for us by a Police Sergeant—after being told by George, our driver, that he had Elizabeth on board! This amused George immensely.

We were then taken to an Army Security checkpoint, where we were to enter the tunnel nicknamed The Great North Road. The Army had given us permission to drive right through the Rock. The lighting inside was poor, but the Navy supplemented it by a battery-operated searchlight on the back of the patrol car. It was a fantastic maze of tunnelling and every provision had been made for housing the entire population should the need arise. They could live for weeks within the security of the Rock.

When we left, we drove to the jetty of the Naval dockyard and through another Security checkpoint to watch a frigate of the Royal Navy leave for home, flying its 'pay off' penant. This was a very impressive sight with the entire crew standing to attention on deck. This formality dates back a long way and was meant to prove that they were entering or leaving a harbour with peaceful intentions. Our escort stood beside the patrol car also at attention, but Janet got so excited she waved, and was rewarded by a very hearty acknowledgement from the Captain himself. Our escort told us that he knew of our presence at the quayside.

A delicious tea had been organised for us all and the boys were most entertaining. They were especially amusing about their reasons for not going to sea, although they were all in the Navy. I think they were enjoying themselves as much as we were.

The Second Officer was on the tender to meet us and helped to carry me up to the top deck again. We had had such a happy day and I felt very sad when they gave me a farewell salute.

The crew had had shore leave for the first time for weeks, and many of them were in no fit state to do any work that evening. The next day, the Captain gave them a public reprimand over the intercom, and said there were six per cent defaulters!

There was a feeling of anticlimax and sadness as the cruise drew to an end. The weather gradually became colder as we neared home waters and we had to start packing. I always hated saying goodbye and felt weepy and depressed. We had made more wonderful friends. The Captain and his crew, passengers and even complete strangers had combined to give me a holiday I shall remember all my life.

We docked at Southampton early in the morning and all the time I was being washed and dressed, people popped into my cabin to say goodbye. The Customs officials were the last of our visitors, until Ron turned up at eleven o'clock with the ambulance. He was utterly exhausted, as he had been on duty all the previous night. Sheila travelled back to

Dover with me, whilst Janet went back to London on the train.

We reached the Isolation Hospital at about six in the evening, and then Ron took Sheila and saw her safely installed in the train, with the clothes basket she had bought at the little store in the Druz village many thousands of miles away.

We had kept a diary each day, otherwise I think I would have doubted the reality of this wonderfully exciting trip.

10

A PLACE OF MY OWN

I DID not remain in the clouds for long as there was much to do that summer getting the flat ready for occupation. The architect who had converted The Old School House for my parents, supervised the structural alterations and various adaptations for me, and with considerable ingenuity, managed to fit all my equipment and apparatus into a very limited space. Overhead rail tracks fitted to stout wooden beams were built across the bedroom and bathroom ceilings. Along these slid a hoist with strong nylon slings, tailored to fit my body, enabling me to be lifted by one person. This gadget has been invaluable and has made nursing much less arduous.

Furnishing the flat meant endless shopping expeditions from the hospital. I was appalled at the high prices and the poor quality of goods displayed, and amazed that department stores took it for granted that people would be willing to wait at least three months for delivery. I realised how very out of touch I had become with modern life. Everything I liked was expensive so I started with the absolute minimum.

Delays were many, but throughout those months of waiting, my father was most helpful and took many of the burdens from my shoulders. He and my mother were as thrilled as I at the prospect of a more normal life in a home of my own. We were under no delusions, however, about the difficulty of finding staff. All of us realised that the success of this venture would depend on finding the right people to look after me. Nowadays, people do not want to be tied down in a residential post and those who applied were looking for a home for themselves. They showed no interest in the job itself.

I had not anticipated defeat at this early stage and it looked as though the whole scheme was going to collapse. The family conferred with Dr. Lynch and Matron, who suggested that if I could find part-time help, I could spend my days at the flat and my nights at the Isolation Hospital. This I did, and towards the end of August, started life as a commuter.

This would be quite an exhausting way of living after my quiet existence at the hospital, and I wondered if I would be able to stand the pace. I knew I could organise and run my own home, but would I get the necessary helpers? Only time would tell. Half an hour after leaving hospital, I was being pushed through my own front door into my own home. It was a thrilling moment. Small luxuries seemed sumptuous after the austerity of hospital life. They gave me tremendous pleasure.

Jane, my first helper, was there to welcome me. There were vases of flowers, and greetings cards from some of my neighbours who had had some doubtful moments as they watched the adaptations proceeding on the ground floor. In spite of my father's explanations to them, they *must* have wondered what sort of a person was coming to live there. I was from the infectious diseases hospital and their knowledge of poliomyelitis was practically non-existent, as was seen when some technicians came to fix my equipment in the flat. They arrived in a white van, on the side of which were the words 'Polio Research Fund'. One of my neighbours dashed out and asked, 'Are you anything to do with antivivisection? Because if you are, we don't approve!'

There is often a certain amount of prejudice against the disabled based on fear and ignorance. On one occasion when I tried to rent a flat, the Committee turned me down, saying I would be converting it into a nursing home. On another occasion, a petition was sent to the property owners suggesting that it would not be hygienic to have someone like me living there. I am thankful to say, however, that my immediate neighbours accepted me with the utmost friendliness and were always ready to help in any way possible. Kind and thoughtful, they contributed, perhaps more than they realised, towards helping me to lead a more normal life.

My flat overlooked the Goodwin Sands, and the part of the English Channel called The Downs where ships often shelter during stormy weather. This is one of the busiest shipping lanes in the world so my view was constantly changing and of immense interest as giant tankers, passenger liners and cargo ships of all kinds passed my windows. Nearer the shore there were small fishing boats and colourful sailing dinghies from the local yacht club. The sea was forever changing—one day grey and stormy with giant waves leaping high over the shingle, and the next calm and of an almost Mediterranean blue. I never tired of watching it.

At first, Ron and his colleagues drove me, but fitting this in with their ambulance duties became impossible. I advertised locally for a first-class driver and found two within reasonable distance of my garage and, for a few weeks, everything ran smoothly. Quite suddenly, one of them went abroad and the other had to go into hospital. I was put in touch with the W.V.S. who produced, as if by magic, a rota of Trinity House Pilots. These men go to sea for a few days of each week, guiding ships safely through the Channel or across to France. Four of them drove me, all very different personalities, making the journey for me a pleasant social half-hour. They were excellent drivers, and though they had had little or no contact with other disabled people, they handled me with the utmost competence and I felt completely safe in their hands. They worked voluntarily and willingly and I never missed a day at the flat or an outing for want of a driver. One of their wives also helped with the driving on the rare occa-

A PLACE OF MY OWN

sions when they were all at sea together and, unless the road was blocked by snow, I was daily transported to my home.

The staff at the hospital were most co-operative and I rarely kept my drivers waiting. This punctuality was invaluable and enabled me to fit in a certain amount of work each day.

It took several weeks to gather all my possessions together under one roof. For twelve years they had been scattered amongst the family and it was exciting to see my treasures, books and pictures again.

Specially designed equipment was installed by the P.O.S.M. (Patient Operated Selector Mechanism) Research Team, which was adapted by the use of electronics. I can operate it simply by sucking and puffing on a mouthpiece, and in this way, manage to ring a bell, switch on and off a light, a fan, a heater, a radio and a television; tilt my bed up and down and use a tape-recorder

My telephone, adapted from a G.P.O. loudspeaker phone is fitted on to a trolley so that it can be used in either lounge or bedroom. It runs off the main electricity supply, but if this failed, a battery automatically takes over, thus keeping me always in touch with the outside world. To operate this, I suck on a mouthpiece which is placed on a metal arm attached to my chair, and speak through a small microphone fitted just above this. To terminate a call, all I have to do is another suck on the mouthpiece. This is expensive equipment to run, but it is certainly one of my most used gadgets. Besides the luxury and joy of direct and easy contact with family and friends, I am able to do my own shopping, organise my staff rotas and, should the need arise, summon immediate assistance.

The P.O.S.M. Research Team are to be congratulated on the work they have done for the totally paralysed. These brilliant inventions make such a difference to our lives. No equipment can replace the human help we need, but it does ease the nurses' burden and gives us independence and security in a way hitherto impossible. My gadgets have become such an integral part of my daily life, that I cannot imagine how I would manage without them.

My painting easel was redesigned by a friend and fitted with an electric motor so that, at the touch of a button, I can move my canvas up, down and sideways, and am able to work on a slightly larger scale.

Now that I had a place of my own, I tried to organise my daily routine to fit in as much work as possible. As soon as I arrive, my equipment is set out for me and I get down to it straight away. I try to calm down and compose my thoughts, but as with all creative activity, inspiration is a very elusive gift, and on the days when it evades me completely, I feel I have wasted valuable time and energy.

Time is a very precious commodity, and dove-tailing my arrangements to fit in with the hospital schedule makes my working hours far too short. I am constantly racing against the clock. Why do I do it? It would be so much easier to sit back and enjoy a life of leisure. I only know that idleness is irksome and happiness for me comes with active creativity. I work to appease my still restless body and to satisfy the inner longings of my soul.

When I bought the flat, it was to become my studio and my office, a place where I could work in peace and in solitude. I have acquired a measure of privacy but not as much as I would like. It may seem ungrateful to want those who help me out of the way, and not everyone understands my need for uninterrupted seclusion during my working hours. Sometimes in spite of broad hints and direct requests, I am faced with the problem—should I be rude but honest? Or should I stop work?

Total reliance on others has been one of the hardest

factors to accept, and probably few people can realise how tedious and exhausting the daily round can be when one always has to ask and be grateful to someone else for every minute request or insignificant movement—things one normally did without thinking. When there is an unsympathetic or unimaginative nurse on duty, life can be hell, but most people are very understanding and helpful.

I am well aware of my many failings. I have always been quick-tempered and intolerant, expecting perfection from myself and others. In the ballet, I was trained to think rapidly and respond immediately to a command and I always seem to be a jump ahead of those looking after me. My brain continues to work exceedingly quickly and I am inclined to forget that nurses are not ballet dancers.

At first sight, ballet training would seem a most unsuitable preparation for a life of immobility, but it gave me a strength and tenacity of purpose I would not otherwise have had. Every day, a dancer tries to perform physical movements that ordinarily seem impossible. The degree of battle to achieve perfection varies with each individual, according to their physique. I had not been born with a ballerina's body, and for me, the going had always been tough.

My father died in July 1966 and I lost my most constant supporter. His health had been failing throughout the year and he had had to spend much of his time in bed. He found it very irksome to be an invalid and we were all profoundly grateful that his suffering was not prolonged. My illness had caused him much anxiety and when his prayers for my recovery were answered, I was told that he suffered agonies of doubt as to whether he had asked too much of God. When I started to paint, however, his doubts were swept away. 'This', he said, 'is the miracle I have waited for', and he was able to rejoice with me in my new-found career.

For a while, I had no heart to paint and when I started

again, I had to work hard in order to complete the Christmas card designs for that year and to fulfil various other commissions. The muscles in my neck became overstrained and I found it impossible to control my paint brush. It just would *not* do what I wanted it to, and technically, I was back to where I started in 1957. X-rays showed no bone malformation and the diagnosis was muscular strain. The orthopaedic Specialist ordered manipulative treatment, physiotherapy and a prolonged rest from painting.

I can only rest my neck muscles when I am in my cuirass at night. During the day, they work continuously to enable me to breathe. In a few weeks, however, the treatment had eased the pain, but when I tried to paint, the brush was as jerky and uncontrolled as before. Was this to be the end of my career as a painter? My ballet career was abruptly ended when I caught polio in 1953. Now fourteen years later, during which time I had struggled to become an artist, it looked as though I was going to have to find yet another outlet for my creative energies.

To prevent myself from thinking too much about my disappointment, I started to write this book. For years, the idea had hovered in the back of my mind and I had made one or two tentative starts, but with the temporary suspension of my artistic pursuits, it seemed that Providence was directing me to get on with it. Inspiration invariably came in the middle of the night when I was not distracted with thoughts of breathing and had uninterrupted peace and quiet. I had no means of recording these ideas though, and often failed to recapture them in the morning. It has been a tremendously stimulating challenge, however, and I have enjoyed creating in a new medium.

11

FULL CIRCLE

FAMILY arrangements made it necessary for me to leave Kent and go and live nearer my sisters in Essex. The thought of uprooting myself and starting again appalled me. My mother was ageing and no longer fit enough to be left on her own. She was going to live with Janet and David and we knew she would only settle down if I moved too. I was in a comfortable rut and did not want to shift.

I had been at the Isolation Hospital for ten years: the staff knew my routine thoroughly; my team of helpers at the flat and the drivers who took me there each day, helped me to run my life in a smooth and orderly fashion. They were all conversant with my ways and equipment, which enabled me to fit in a considerable amount of work each day. I felt no enthusiasm at all for the terrific upheaval facing me. The whole thing seemed formidable and far beyond my strength.

Looking at it dispassionately, however, it was obviously a wise move, whatever the cost, and as soon as I had made up my mind, it was surprising how things fell into place. I was offered a bed at Broomfield Hospital near Chelmsford, and my sister Brighid found a delightful little house not far away. I would still be a daily commuter, but the journey would be shorter and less tiring. Negotiations for the sale were carried through remarkably quickly, and by the end of November, I had sold my flat and moved.

Deep down, I was confident I was doing the right thing, but it was a terrible wrench leaving everyone, and only by intensified work could I keep myself from dwelling on it too much. I was dependent on so many people for so much and

I knew I was going to miss them. The future was full of unknown quantities; the same problems loomed before me as I had faced when I bought the flat three years ago. Would my equipment fit into the new house? Would the hospital be co-operative and allow me a longer day at home? Would I get drivers for my ambulance? And would I get staff to help me at home? I felt I was launching myself into a void.

It was sad seeing the flat dismantled, and I left my helpers to supervise the actual moving of the furniture after I had left. Ron, and a colleague of his, John, packed all my equipment into my ambulance and a van. The Isolation Hospital had not looked so tidy since I moved in ten years ago.

We drove direct to Broomfield. On arrival, the head Porter asked me for a letter of identification. I looked at my packed ambulance and at John, barely visible beneath all my equipment. A note of introduction seemed rather superfluous. Hospitals would be very over-crowded if all their patients arrived as I did. Janet Harvey came with me and stayed at the hospital for the first three nights. This was a tremendous help, as she was able to explain my equipment to the nurses and show them my rather intricate routine.

Broomfield Hospital is the old T.B. sanitorium situated in beautiful grounds. It is built in a V-shape and gets the sun all day long. There are over fifty beds in Ward I, in single and double cubicles, opening on to wide, light corridors which extend as far as the eye can see. The nurses must have to walk miles whilst on duty. I was put in No. 6, a large, single cubicle, newly decorated in the same colour pink I had left in Dover. The whole of one wall was a folding glass door, opening on to the terrace which overlooked the garden. It was a lovely view—not a house in sight. My equipment followed, and as usual, overflowed into the corridor, immediately making the place look untidy. Sister was charming about it, however, and Janet quickly sorted it out and tried to make it look a little less. I said goodbye to my drivers. Ron had been with me for eight years and I knew he would be very hard to replace.

After lunch, two of the P.O.S.M. Research Team came to fix up my equipment. Their greeting at the hospital entrance had been, 'What are you then, Pest Control?'

I thought I had made the place look untidy, but when they started work, it looked as though a demolition squad had hit the room. The staff took it all quite calmly, and by about 6.30 p.m., everything was tidied up and in working order. Brighid and her children called to see me. They told me that, at the house, the builder had already put up the beams for my hoist and the G.P.O. had installed my special telephone—magnificent co-operation.

A house is not quite as practical as a flat or a bungalow for someone in a wheelchair, but it was the only suitable property we could find in the district. It is set in its own grounds with a fairly large garden at the back. Brighid had arranged for me to interview some staff there on the following afternoon. It was empty except for a couple of deck chairs and some utensils for making tea, but the central heating was on and the place was warm.

Matron and the ward Sister had discussed my daily routine and decided that I could leave hospital at 9.30 in the morning and return at 8 o'clock at night. This gave me a longer day and sounded eminently satisfactory and I planned accordingly. I employed two very charming helpers and was able to start at my house at the beginning of the week.

As I write this now, there is still much to do to get things in perfect running order. A start has been made and I hope the hardest part is behind me. I need more help, but it often comes from the most unexpected quarters. For instance, some members of the Fire Brigade offered to drive my ambulance in their spare time. In the first week, they had organised themselves into a rota and completely eliminated my transport problems.

One of the biggest attractions about moving had been the possibility that I might teach dancing again. I had already given my nieces classes in National and ballet. They had responded well, which was very rewarding, and they had obviously enjoyed them as they kept asking for more. I found it exhausting and sometimes exasperating, trying to explain movements verbally. It is very much easier to demonstrate them, especially to beginners. When things really got beyond me, Brighid, who is also a dancer, would come to my assistance and between us, we conveyed my ideas to the children. When the local ballet company asked me to set a Tarantella for eight girls for their forthcoming show, I accepted the challenge, and less than a week after I arrived in Chelmsford, I took my first rehearsal.

There were plenty of willing hands to lift me up the steps into the ballet room. As the girls changed into their tights and tunics, they cast shy glances in my direction. I think they wondered how somebody like me could teach them to dance. For my part, I was wondering if I could make them understand and interpret my choreography. Brighid had done the auditioning and preliminary teaching, and was there to demonstrate if my explanations proved inadequate. We had worked the whole dance out on paper when I stayed with her in the summer, but I must confess I had forgotten quite a lot of it. My biggest problem, however, was a broken joist which made the floor rock alarmingly, and at times I was nearly shaken out of my chair.

The dance is now taking shape and I am amazed how quickly the girls grasp my ideas, how readily they respond to correction and how much they appear to enjoy the rehearsals. Occasionally, dancing is too subtle to put into words; then, I feel my helplessness. I grope around for the right word or a vague comparison; I watch the class hoping for an inkling of the right movement, and unless someone produces this and I can work on it, I am defeated. Then I long for an active body so that I can show them just what I mean. These moments of defeat are rare. Most movements can be explained in words, though I think many people find it harder to listen and learn, as they are so used to copying what they see.

I have always loved teaching and it is wonderful to be back in the ballet world again. I have no illusions about it however. It is hard work—for me, very hard work, and I know I have not the stamina to do more than a few hours a week. But, in spite of my years away from it all, I have forgotten very little. And I long, as all teachers do, to pass my knowledge and experience on to others.

If anybody had told me a few years ago that I would be teaching dancing again today, I would not have believed them. Yet it feels quite normal for me to be doing so, and often I become so engrossed in it that I forget my disability altogether. Painting, writing, teaching dancing—what's next I wonder?

12

EPILOGUE

People often ask me if my experiences have left any bitterness in my mind. I can honestly answer that I do not think they have. When I was in the iron lung, the future certainly looked grim. My career as a ballet dancer had been suddenly terminated and before me stretched a life of immobility, a life of helplessness and utter dependence on others. It took me about four years to get over my depression and disappointment, and to adjust myself to a new way of life.

I was the least medically minded member of my family and had always shunned illness and deformity. But, here I was, plunged in at the deep end. Why did it have to happen to me; I do not know. I do not know why I was afflicted with total paralysis. I do not believe there is a purpose discoverable behind this happening, but I do believe that it is God's will that I should accept it with graciousness and equanimity, and do as much as I can with my life in spite of my disability.

Often, I feel angry and frustrated, intolerant and disappointed, but I hope I am never bitter. Bitterness is self-destructive. It goes with self-pity, and neither of these qualities are pleasant to live with.

Perhaps if I had been involved in an accident I might have felt bitterness towards those responsible, but it was nobody's fault that I got polio and I certainly do not feel angry with the Almighty because of what has happened to me. I accept it as a kind of challenge, a testing of my strength of faith and will.

The discipline has been good for me and I sense that, as a

result of it, I am a better person than I was before I was ill.

Of course, I realise that I am luckier than many other disabled people. First, I live in a country with a magnificent standard of medical and welfare services. For years I have received, free of charge, devoted care and attention, but I have had much more than this. Many in the profession have gone far beyond their medical duties and have given, unstintingly, their time to encourage, help and advise me on all kinds of subjects.

Secondly, I have not been burdened with a deteriorating illness. Though polio left me very severely disabled, I know I will get no worse, and this knowledge makes it easier to accept it.

Thirdly, I have a wonderful family and a large circle of friends, from whom I receive more than my fair share of love and help.

Lastly, though much was taken from me, much has been given in return. I have been able to express myself in paint and words, and to return to the world of ballet and the work I love.

Work has been the most valuable asset in my life. Not only has it given me an aim and purpose for living, but it has also provided me with a much needed creative outlet and a means whereby I can spend part of my day away from hospital. Determination, will-power and constant effort are needed on my part, but only with the co-operation of others can I achieve results. So far a steady stream of willing people has come to my aid. Was it luck, coincidence, or Providence that, at each stage of my career, the right person has turned up to help me at precisely the right moment?